Joyce Liao

Be a Dance Artist Your Own Way

– *Strength, Beauty, Freedom, and Creativity*

Foreword by Ailin Chiu

My gratitude to those who have guided and supported me
in my dance journey.

Contents

Foreword 1

Preface 3

1 You Hold The Magic Wand Of Dance 6

2 Make Creativity A Daily Habit 12

3 Love And Nurture Your Inner Artist 22

4 Stay Healthy: Avoid Destructive Self-criticism 30

5 Dance To Boost Your Self-confidence 40

6 Keep An Open Mind 48

7 Having Diverse Skills Can Help You Succeed 58

8 Establish Your Own Learning Schedule 66

9 Find Your Artistic Voice 74

10 Body Inclusivity: Embrace & Love Your Body 82

11 What Are Your Dance Goals 94

References 105

Image Credits 109

About the Author 111

Foreword

By Ailin Chiu -

A freelance journalist and a dear friend of the author.

"Be a Dance Artist Your Own Way" is an exceptional self-help book that offers invaluable guidance and insights to those embarking on a journey in dance. Authored by Joyce Liao, this remarkable guide serves as an empowering resource for aspiring dancers and individuals seeking personal growth through the art of movement.

What sets this book apart is its ability to address the multi-faceted challenges faced by dancers, going beyond mere technical instruction to explore the deeper aspects of self-discovery. Through insightful anecdotes and practical exercises, the book delves into the importance of self-confidence, self-expression, and self-care, providing readers with indispensable tools for success.

One of the book's most remarkable features is its holistic approach to growth. While technical proficiency is important, the author emphasizes the significance of cultivating a versatile skill set and exploring various dance styles. By encouraging readers to step out of their comfort zones and embrace creativity, the book empowers dancers to overcome challenges, unleash their artistic potential, and make informed decisions aligned with their unique artistic vision.

"Be a Dance Artist Your Own Way" is a must-read for anyone passionate about dance and personal growth. With its profound insights, practical advice, and uplifting tone, this book is a trusted guide that empowers dancers to embark on a transformative path of self-discovery through the art of movement. Whether you are a beginner or an experienced dancer, this book will leave a lasting impact on your journey, helping you unlock your true potential as a dancer and as an individual.

Preface

As a dancer and choreographer, I believe that dance is one of the most powerful forms of art that allows individuals to express themselves through movement. After completing my Bachelor of Arts in Dance from the University of Washington, I continued to engage in the creation of my own dances, in addition to having the opportunities to perform in works by other amazing artists. Immersing myself in diverse performance events has allowed me to closely observe the creative processes of fellow artists. Throughout these recent years, I have discovered commonalities within these processes and identified practices that prove notably helpful to artists. I am excited to share my insights into these practices and offer my perspective on the current dance landscape, with the hope that the information will benefit my readers.

Becoming a dancer is a captivating journey, but it is never an easy path. Because of the intense competition in the field, dancers face a lot of stress, both mentally and physically, as they strive to get closer to their dance dreams. The tough competition and pressure often kick in from a young age, making a lasting impact on the artists' careers and life paths.

While there's no quick solution to make the journey of becoming a dancer a breeze, there are savvy steps dancers can take to prepare and empower themselves. By building a strong sense of self-confidence, cultivating one's creativity, and developing diverse skill sets, dancers will be able to come up with creative solutions when confronted with career challenges. Armed with these qualities, they can make well-informed decisions that best serve both themselves and their art.

Traditionally, dancers are expected to devote the majority, if not all, of their time in the dance studio to perfect their technique. However, acquiring skills such as choreography, visual design, videography, writing, or even public speaking and business administration can prove incredibly beneficial. Developing diverse skills in different areas can enhance the ability to think creatively and solve problems – traits that are extremely valuable in any career and the rapidly evolving world that we live in today. The interdisciplinary intelligence that one has gained in the process can create new opportunities, and it will prove especially helpful while navigating challenging situations.

When life presents us with precious opportunities, we bravely step forward. When life gives us lemons, we gracefully make lemonade. By writing this book, I aim to share practices that I believe are essential for dancers – practices that contribute to both the artistic and life journeys of individuals. In my experience, winning dance competitions does not automatically make someone a great dancer. A truly great dancer is a brave and enlightened artist, always ready to thrive with strength, beauty, freedom, and creativity, regardless of life's challenges.

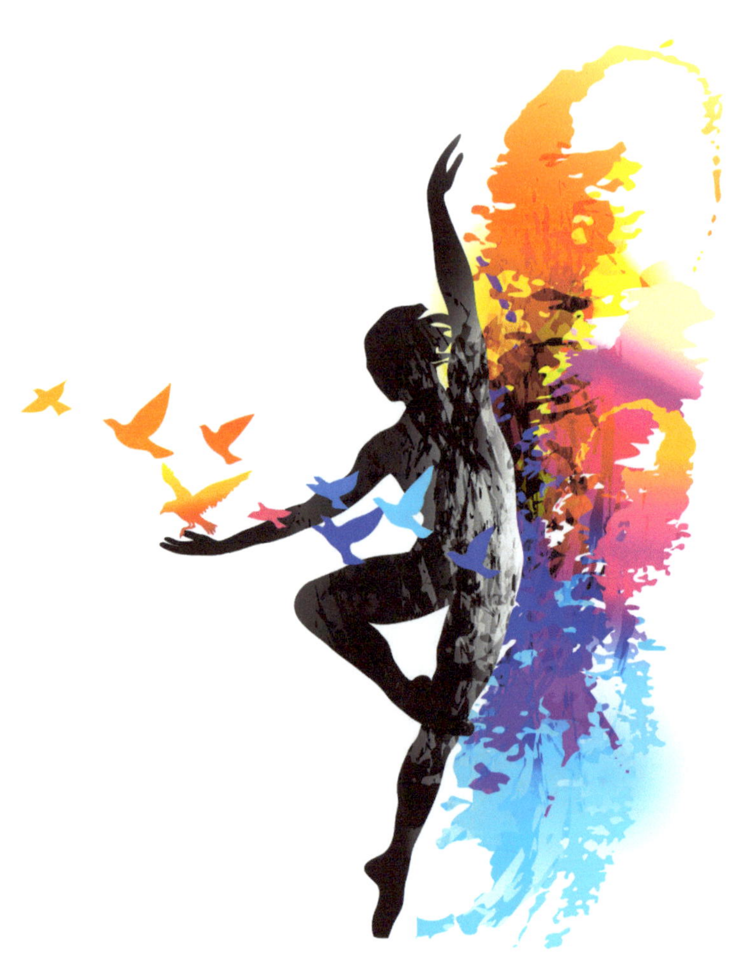

1 You Hold The Magic Wand Of Dance

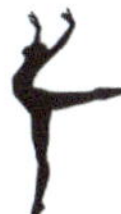

A lot of us began dancing because we saw dance performances that inspired us – whether it was an online video, a Nutcracker ballet, a community theater, or a mind-blowing performance by someone we knew. My own dream for the longest time was to become a star dancer in a dance company that would travel the world, delivering the most spectacular performances.

Following the traditional path of a dance career by joining a major dance company is a common dream for many young and aspiring dancers. However, it may not always be the most suitable choice due to reasons such as intense competition in the field, body-type restrictions, limited creative freedom within a company, or age considerations. Fortunately, pursuing a traditional dance career is not the only way to achieve great dance performances and make a dancer's dream come true.

As I matured and gained more exposure to various creative processes in dance, I discovered that great dances can be made even without the backing of an established dance company. There are many alternative avenues for independent dancers and freelance artists to explore, allowing them to find their unique strengths and voices in the process of producing new dance works.

How is it possible to create great dances without the support of an established dance institution? This is achievable simply because the source of dance magic comes from **within the dancers themselves**. When dancers have a dance floor, creativity, courage, and skills they need, they can make great dances happen!

Many important elements constitute a dance performance that we see on a stage, including sound design, stage design, lighting design, costume design, makeup design, etc. However, among various aspects of a performance, a dancer's presence, energy, and artistic articulation are the most essential. Audiences often share the experience of being absorbed by a dancer's strong stage presence or persona. When this happens, we say that the audience is **inspired by the dancer**. This dancer's presence or persona is the most powerful element of a performance – it is **the soul of a dance**. This is true for street, tap, jazz, lyrical, and ballroom dance. This is true even for classical ballet, which usually holds some of the strictest forms and standards.

What was your most profound experience seeing a dance performance? What was so special about it?

When a dancer appears on stage, they can immediately transform the stage into a story scene or a transcended landscape through the power of their presence and artistic expression. In the ballet *Giselle*, when the spirit of Giselle rises from her grave as a spirit to meet Prince Albrecht, she embodies the divine feminine, full of calm, love, and forgiveness. Her white translucent skirt, the music, and the stage lights all help create this unforgettable scene, but the most powerful element is the ballerina's presence. Through imagination and the power of the mind, a great dancer can embody 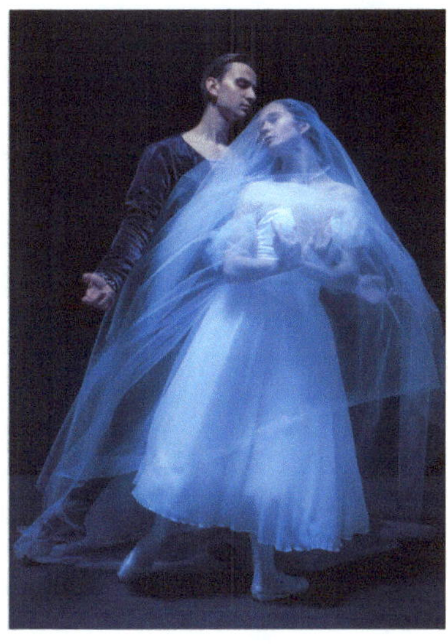 the character of a story, transform the performance space, and bring the most profound experience to their audience. This is a dancer's magic to transform and transcend!

How would you describe the magical feeling when you dance? Do you get this feeling every time you dance?

This **power to transform and transcend** is a dancer's magic wand. It is what allows a dancer, or any good performing artist, to create sparks and magic in their art. Some dancers describe the feeling of this transcendence as "being part of something bigger than oneself." Some people describe it as a feeling of complete freedom or being able to fully express one's true self. Agnes de Mille made this famous statement: "To dance is to be out of yourself, larger, more powerful, more beautiful." No matter how you describe it, this power to transcend comes from within a dancer. It is part of a dancer's heart and soul that's being seen and felt by the audience during a performance. A dancer's magic belongs uniquely to the dancer, and it can never be stolen or taken away by anybody else.

With sufficient training and practice, dancers can exercise their magic to transform and transcend from anywhere – not just on a performance stage. You can become a fairy queen/king on a grand stage or in a private rehearsal studio. You can do it in an outdoor park or comfortably at your favorite creative corner. A stage is a good option, but it is not the only option. Dance magic should not be confined to stages that are always controlled under busy production schedules. When dance artists follow their inspiration, they can bring forth dances in various forms and spaces, whether it is for art performance, healing, personal exploration, or community bonding.

Do you have a favorite dance space outside the school or company studio? (Hint: This place may not always have a Marley floor and a huge mirror. It can be any space where you feel safe and comfortable to move around or test out your new movement ideas.)

Dance is an art that breathes its own life. As dance artists, our job is to channel that inspiration and allow ourselves to be led by it.

With creativity, skills, and willingness to try, there will be many ways to experience the power and beauty of dance. Once we understand the power we hold, there will be endless possibilities and adventures for us to explore. If you are a dancer, the magic wand of dance is right here in your hand. You hold the magical connection between this dance inspiration and the world we live in. The connection you hold serves as the ultimate source of power and beauty in the art of dance.

Dancers have the power to make dance happen, wherever they want, however they want!

The power to transform and transcend is a dancer's magic wand. This power allows a dancer, or any good performing artist, to create sparks and magic in their art.

2 Make Creativity A Daily Habit

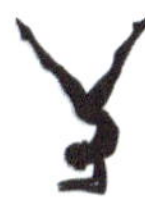

We should try to make art as often as we can. Artists make a living by creating and selling their art. However, even if you don't need to sell your artwork for cash, making art and engaging in creativity are some of the best things any person can do to brighten their days and make their life more fulfilling. Contrary to the old belief that only a creative genius can make good art, we should realize that each of us has a creative genius living inside us. To get in touch with our inner creative genius, we need to take every chance to practice artmaking and be creative as often as possible. We need to **make creativity a daily habit**.

Scientists have proved that artmaking is extremely beneficial to one's mental health and well-being. A study conducted by Ravn and Høffding, published in the American Psychological Association, has demonstrated that creative activities can help reduce stress and anxiety, improve mood, and increase feelings of social connectedness [1]. There are many forms of creativity in art. Some familiar ones include drawing, painting, poetry writing, songwriting, photography, and, of course, dancemaking! Committing time to creativity regularly can help us feel more connected to our inner selves and our surroundings. It is a wonderful, healthy, and exhilarating way to enhance the quality of our daily lives.

What are your favorite creative activities? Do you commit regular time to these activities?

As dancers, we should feel empowered to be as creative as possible with dance. In a dance class, a teacher or a choreographer usually has the steps ready for us. Instead of deciding what we want to dance or how we want to express ourselves, we are given a set of instructions and steps to follow. Even though performing other people's work can be a great learning experience, we should also take opportunities to create our own dances whenever possible. There is a great bonus when you are a dancer with choreographic or improvisational skills – you can create your own dances!

Dance improvisation is a wonderful way to tap into one's creative juice. To "improv" is to move freely and spontaneously without rigid pre-planning or choreography. Sheets-Johnstone describes dance improvisation as a kind of dancing that "lives and breathes in the moving flow of its creation". It is a process that involves a non-separation of thinking and doing [2]. Dance improvisation can be seen as a standalone practice or a form of performance. It can also be done in conjunction with other creative mediums, such as being part of a multidisciplinary art installation. It's worth mentioning that the longstanding tradition of applying improvisation has extended across numerous art forms, including theater, music, poetry, performance art, as well as the visual arts. Curtis Carter, a professor of Philosophy at Marquette University, explained that in a broader cultural context, improvisation signified the rejection of hierarchical practices in pre-planned performances and the embrace of **open forms** in art where "the process became more important than the final product" [3].

In addition to being a standalone practice or a form of performance, dance improvisation can serve as a wonderful practice for choreographers and creative workers in various ways. In a study done by dance researchers Dou, Jia, and Ge, it has been proven that dance improvisation is an important method that can help people unleash and develop their creative abilities [4]. It is no surprise, considering how many choreographers today have dance improvisation as their favorite creative tool. Dancers conduct improvisation for various reasons. Some use it for artistic expression, while others seek personal experiences or healing in the process. The beauty of dance improvisation lies in its flexibility – it can be pursued in any manner that resonates with an individual, alone or with a group.

If you can make a new dance, what kind of dance will you create?

If you are new to dance improvisation but eager to dive in, consider focusing on aspects such as:

- » Experience the freedom or sensation of movement (this is essential for **somatic dance practice** [5])
- » Release your emotions in an unhindered way
- » Explore or create new movements
- » Explore or challenge your comfort zones
- » Find in-person connections through **contact improvisation**
- » Find personal healing in **dance therapy**

For a deeper exploration of improvisation, *The Moment of Movement* is an excellent book to start with. In this book, Blom and Chaplin emphasize that the key to improvisation lies in a dancer's willingness to fully commit themselves to the movement, take risks, and authentically respond to their kinesthetic and sensory impulses [6]. All these elements are essential for tapping into one's creativity in dance.

For those who enjoy organization, patterns, and designs, choreography can be an excellent creative practice. **Choreography** trains the way we visualize images, organize movements, and arrange spatial patterns. To choreograph effectively, we also need to be aware of our synchronization with music and rhythms over time and assess whether the dancers' bodies naturally align with the movements. As choreographers, we get the opportunity to develop our unique artistic voices and invent new dance movements.

Choreography can be a rigorous practice, regardless of the type of piece you undertake. For example, crafting a solo dance requires unwavering commitment and intense focus; it necessitates a high degree of self-discipline. On the other hand, choreographing a group dance demands exceptional communication and leadership abilities.

As the choreographer for a group dance, you will need to oversee each dancer, direct rehearsals, collaborate with the production team, and create a new piece – possibly all at the same time. It will require some serious multi-tasking skills.

In the past, dancemaking used to be done only by choreographers or elite dance professionals who had dedicated their entire careers to the art. Today, we are fortunate to have more accessible opportunities. With the abundance of resources that are readily available, everyone with even some dance training can make a dance, and everyone should consider giving it a try.

Dancemaking is not about right or wrong, and it goes beyond judgments of good or bad. Dancemaking is simply a way to open new doors and see how much discovery, creative juice, and fulfillment you can get out of the process. It can be as simple as unwrapping a new box of crayons and starting to enjoy the delightful colors they bring to us. The dancemaking process should be non-stressful, fun, playful, and easy for people to engage in on a regular basis. It should be a healthy and wonderful creativity enjoyed by anyone who wants to do it.

Be it drawing, poetry writing, dance improvisation, or choreography, the more often you engage in these creative activities, the less intimidation you'll feel, and the more freedom you'll discover within them. The best way to think of creativity is to see it as a daily habit that you can enjoy without too much pressure. If you are a dancer and you haven't yet tried to make a dance, don't wait too long to start your creative adventure in dance!

Grab a notebook while you dive into this book! Feel free to write down your thoughts and ideas in your journal – it's a good way to make the most of your reading experience.

1 Ravn, S. & Høffding, S. (2022)

2 Weir, K. (2022, April)

3 Carter, C.L. (2000)

4 Dou, X., Jia, L., and Ge, J. (2021)

5 Batson, G. and the IADMS Dance Educators' Committee (2009)

6 Blom, L.A. & Chaplin, L.T. (1988, December 15)

Dance Notes ~ write down your thoughts!

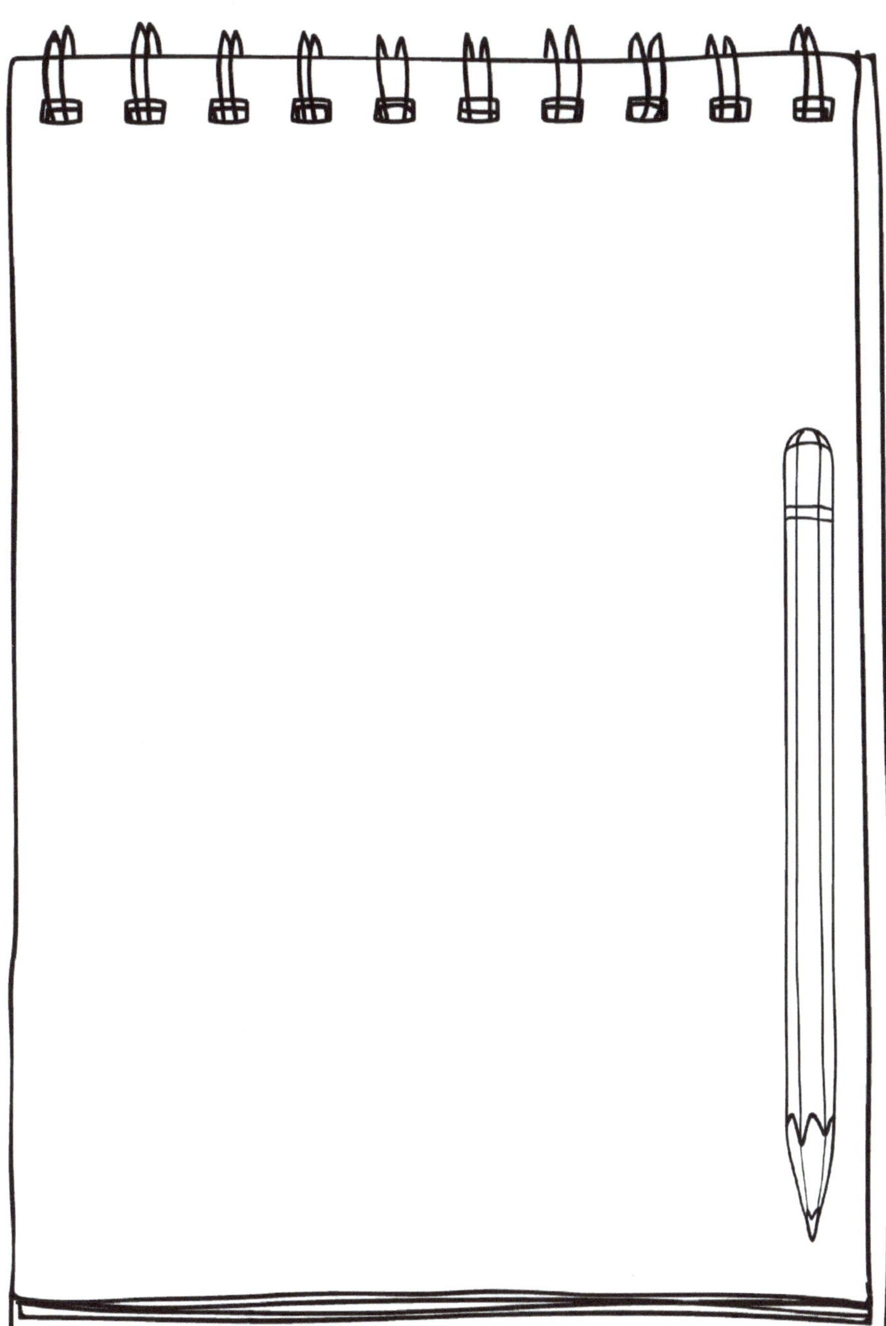

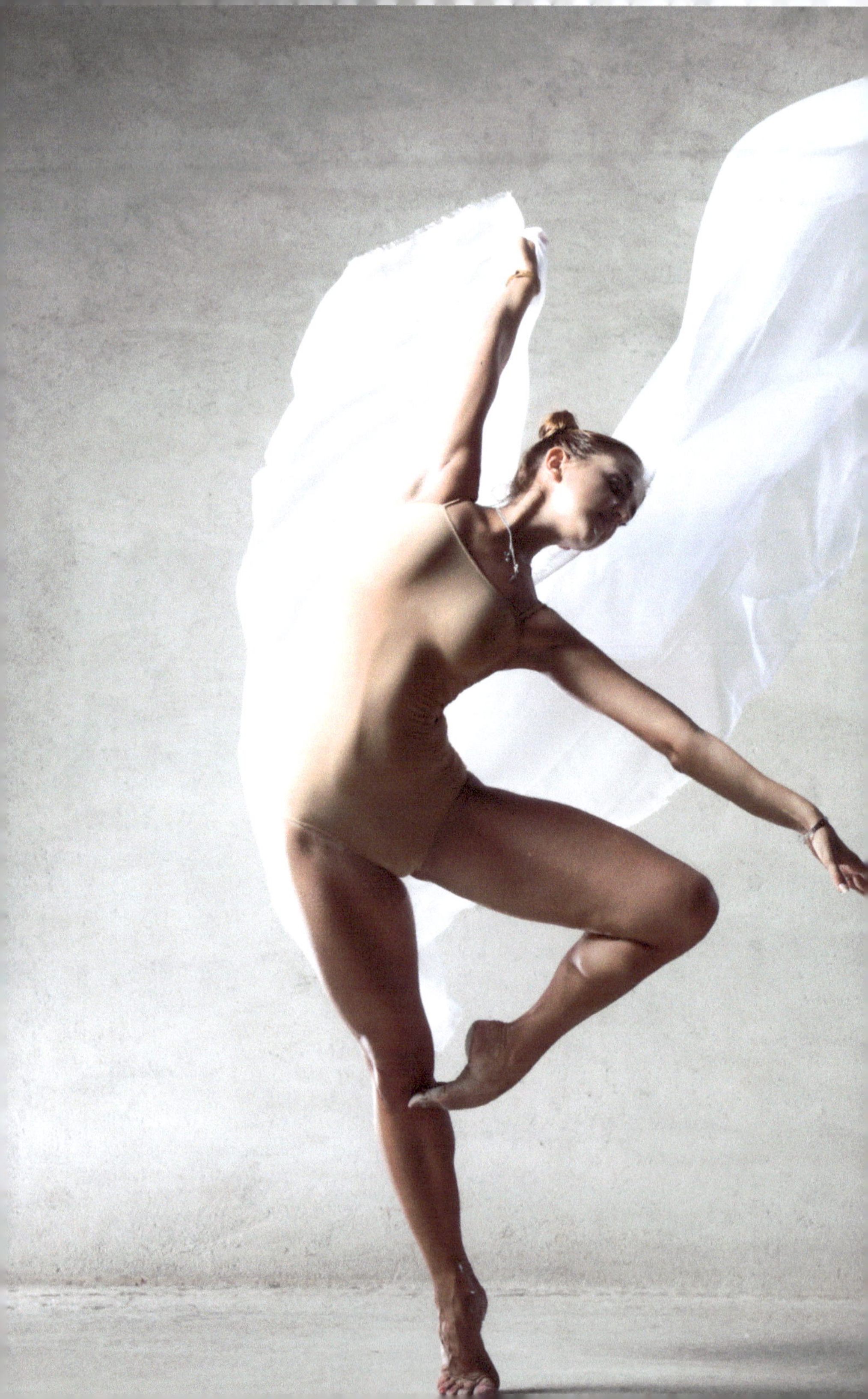

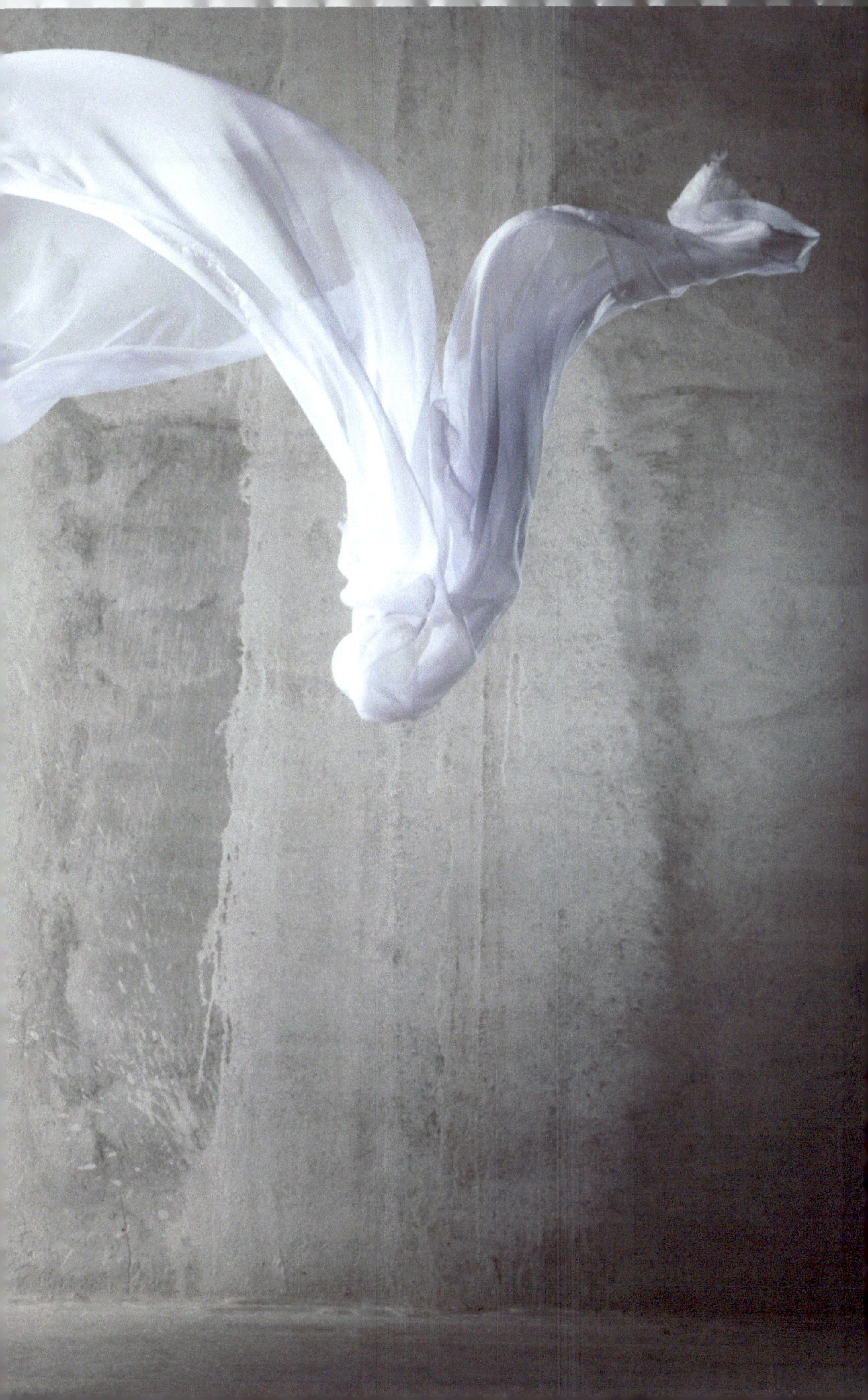

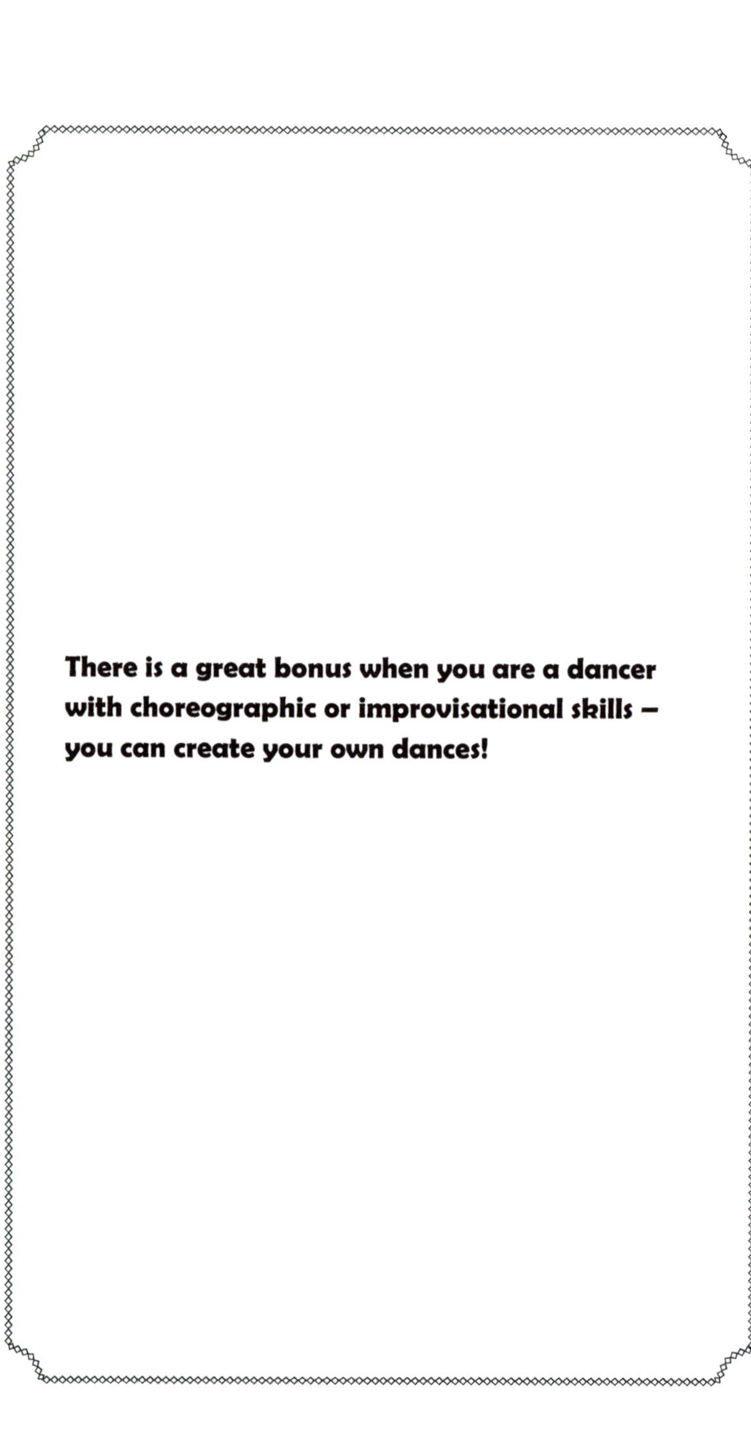

There is a great bonus when you are a dancer
with choreographic or improvisational skills —
you can create your own dances!

3 Love And Nurture Your Inner Artist

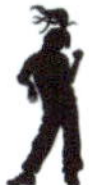

When it comes to creativity, we first need to give ourselves permission to try, experiment, and play. There is an inner artist in each of us. An inner artist is the part of us that is imaginative, expressive, and playful. Similar to the development of any new skills or interests, our inner artists need our acceptance and support to grow. It may take many years for our inner artists to grow strong enough before they can fully manifest their creative potential and artistic prowess.

Like tender-hearted children, our inner artists can be vulnerable and in need of encouragement and nurturing. Many of us in the dance community, particularly those with a ballet background, recognize the importance of honing good dance techniques. However, not enough of us understand the equal importance of safeguarding and uplifting our inner artists to foster creativity in dance. If we want to evolve into dance artists who can freely explore new movements and create new dance works, we need to love and nurture our inner artists from the beginning.

When was the last time you allowed yourself to create something artistically just for the joy of it?

There is a born-to-be artist inside every child. Children can draw, paint, sing, or dance spontaneously. Not only can they make art naturally, but they also have so much fun doing it! When children draw, they don't worry if their skills are good enough or if they have completed the Level-300 class at an art school. They just follow their creative instinct and dive in. In the process of drawing, they focus without needless doubts. They aren't afraid that they will make fools of themselves by drawing something ugly or stupid, and they don't worry about whether they will lose in an art competition next week.

When it comes to dancing, children can start dancing as soon as they feel the beat of the music. Children engage in "dance improvisation" naturally without even knowing it. They don't need rehearsals before dancing to a lovely song in front of their family and friends. As a result, children often have the best time dancing. They can fully enjoy the moment without the fear of being judged. The absence of fear is what allows children to go fully creative and experience immense joy in the process. It is not just little children being cute and naive. What we witness in them is their ability to **follow their innate creativity to make art**.

During our early years, most of us never reached a point where we didn't know how to be creative. The worry-free state of mind as children was what enabled us to enjoy creativity so profoundly. The only time creativity seemed to be "unlearned" was when fear and a lack of self-permission came into play. The ability to connect to one's creative intuition is, in fact, a very crucial step before an individual can engage in any type of creativity in art, including dancemaking. This connection is like **the core engine for any creative mind**. We were all born with this amazing ability to create and make art. However, these precious, potentially delicate, artistic traits need to be encouraged and nurtured over time, regardless of age – whether you're a child or an adult.

Did you lose some of your confidence in creativity as you grew up? What will help you regain the confidence that you once had?

We need to keep telling ourselves that inside each of us, there is an inner artist. Our inner artists harbor the most incredible talents and creative intuition; all they need is the opportunity to grow and flourish over time. Every day, we draw when our inner artists call us to draw, and we dance when they inspire us to move. We must always remain mindful and attentive to the voices of our inner artists, seek to understand their needs, and make efforts to establish stronger connections with them. Only by accepting and nurturing our inner artists with love and care, can we keep our creative channels fully open and continue to enjoy and explore artmaking for as long as we want.

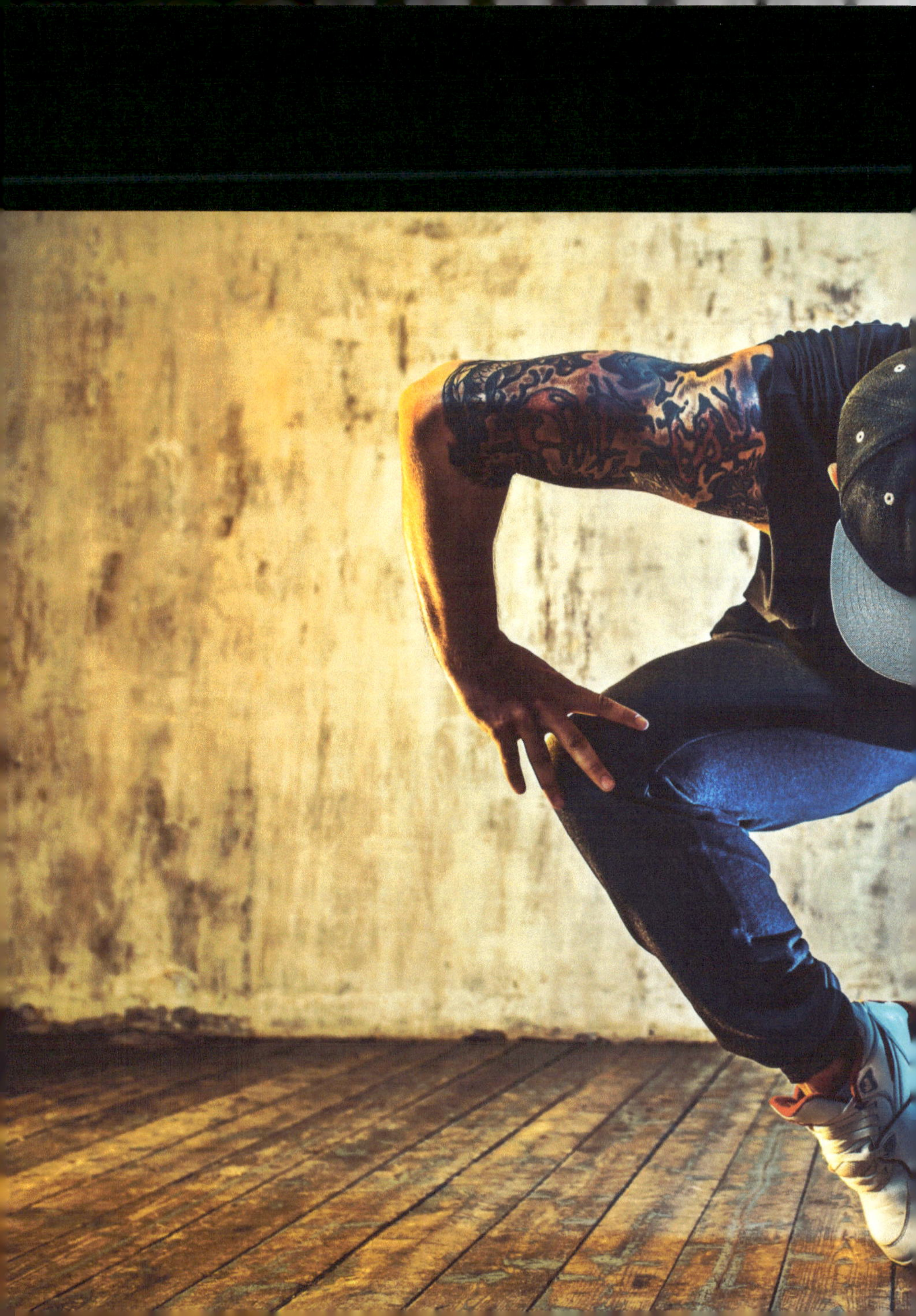

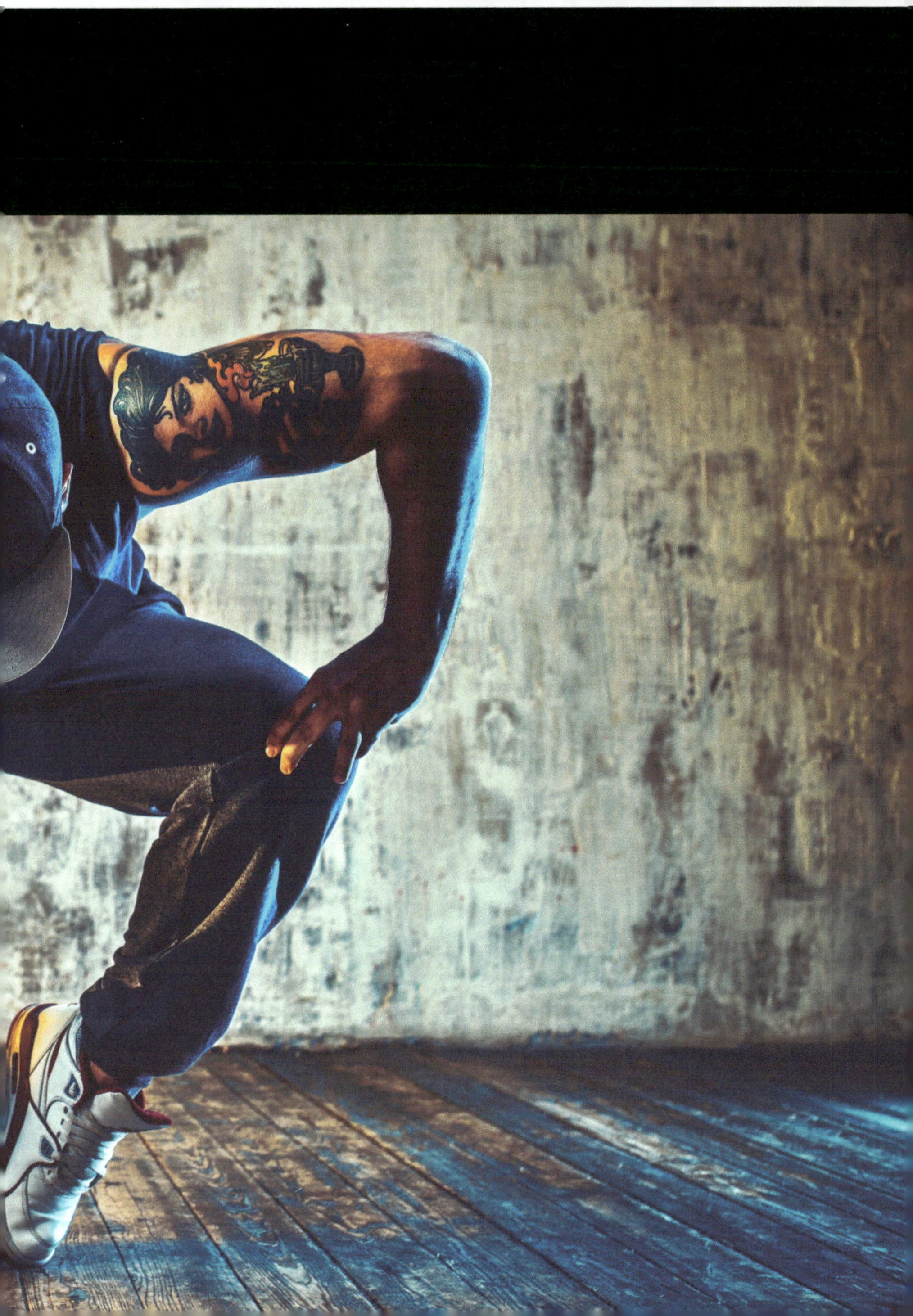

Are you good at connecting with your inner artist? Reflect on when any of the following situations takes place – it may be when your inner artist is trying to speak to you:

◊   Do you sing or dance by yourself just for the joy of it?

◊   Do you allow yourself to make funky movements that are unconventional but interesting?

◊   Does dancing spark your imagination?

◊   Does dancing make you feel especially free or happy?

◊   Do you want to create a completely new and unique dance, unlike anything you've seen before?

Dance Notes ~ write down your thoughts!

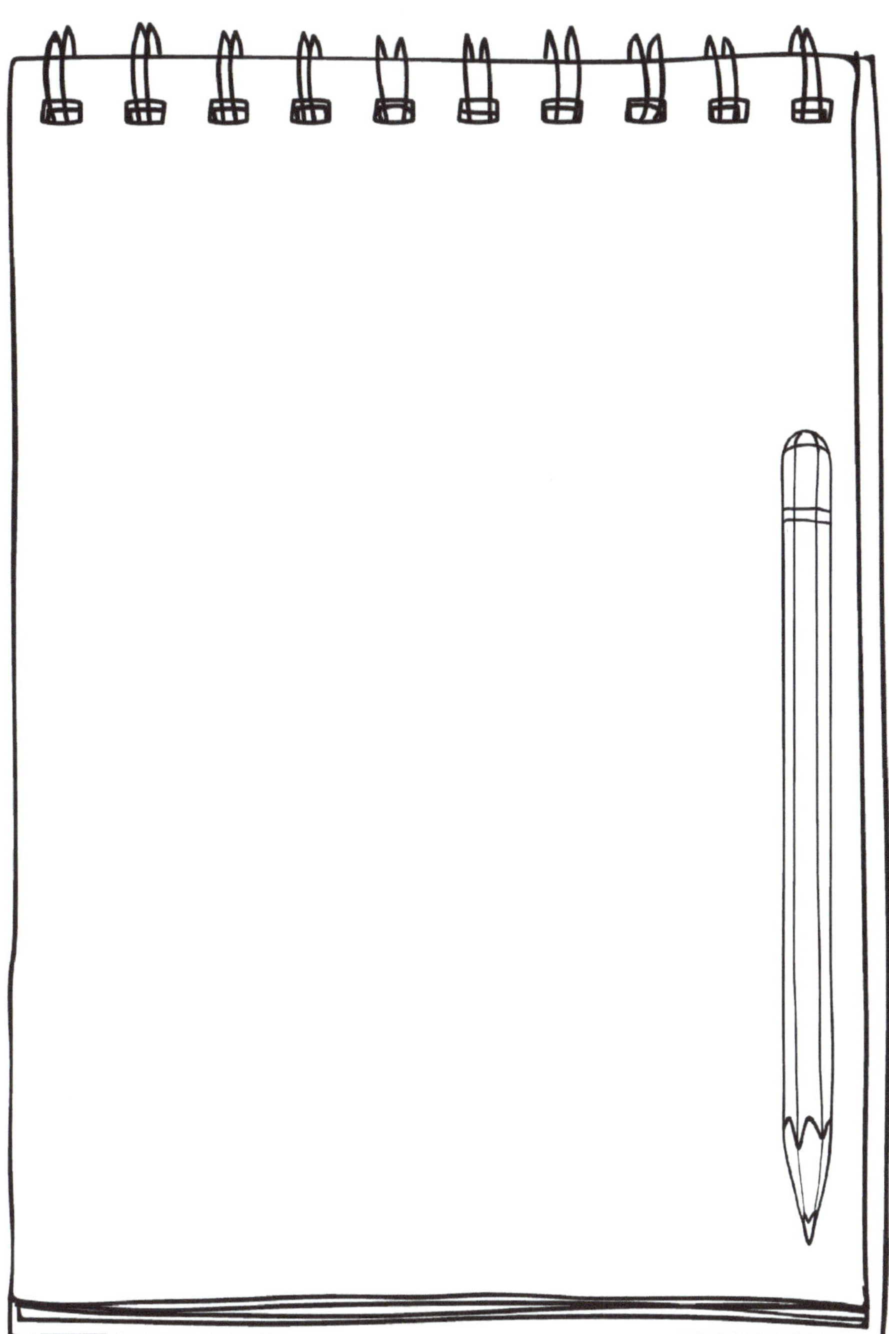

Not enough of us understand the importance of safeguarding and nurturing our inner artists, which is absolutely essential when it comes to fostering creativity in dance.

4 Stay Healthy: Avoid Destructive Self-criticism

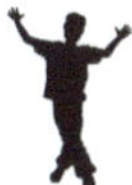

Self-criticism occurs when an individual attempts to censor their own faults or shortcomings. Self-criticism in artmaking is a habit that we have learned as we grow up. **Constructive self-criticism** is task-specific and actionable. It does not stress us out, and it should not push us beyond a reasonable or healthy threshold. A healthy dose of constructive self-criticism will help us improve and achieve higher goals. It is important for any type of learning process. However, too much of a good thing can turn harmful!

Excessive or **destructive self-criticism** in artmaking, as well as in any other field, can be toxic. Over the long term, it can destroy our self-confidence, undermine our creativity, and result in feelings of worthlessness or guilt. Excessive or destructive self-criticism is like a cancer in an artist's development. It is a nasty trickster that first appears as something that will help us improve. Only later do we realize that destructive self-criticism has eroded our confidence and paralyzed our ability to take empowering steps in art.

What were some examples of constructive versus destructive criticism that you had imposed on yourself? How did you differentiate between the two?

We already know that children are fearless artists who can draw with imagination and joy. So, how do they ever lose that confidence? Perhaps after receiving a careless or hurtful comment, a child begins to overly self-criticize or doubt their ability to create something beautiful and amazing again. People's comments can easily impact a child's confidence. Therefore, while honesty is important, we should be mindful of children's feelings in our communication with them. This example highlights that destructive self-criticism is a learned habit, potentially acquired through our imitation and repetition of someone else's critical or negative behavior.

Toddlers' dance videos are so adorable! For those of us who once loved showcasing our brilliant dance moves in front of our parents' cameras, when did some of us become hesitant and shy about dancing in front of others? Perhaps it was after we, regrettably, compared our looks and body types to some commercial impressions and felt unjustly ashamed. They might be the image we glimpsed while passing a fashion billboard, which dazzlingly showcased our favorite cosmetics or outfits brands on models with unrealistically slender body types. The irony was that many of those images weren't even real. Digitally altered and distorted by photo editing software, they were utterly incapable of representing our healthy, real bodies.

Sadly, we wouldn't have known it at the time. It was when some of us started to **_negatively label our bodies_** and believe that we weren't beautiful enough to become great dancers. This pointless comparison and destructive self-criticism can inflict serious damage on our confidence, even to the point of compromising our mental and physical health, leading to illnesses likes depression or eating disorders (see "Chapter 10" about body inclusivity and the risk of eating disorders in dance).

Fortunately, there are cures – The antidotes to self-imposed destructive criticism in dance are **_self-acceptance_** and **_self-permission_**. When the censorious inner critics start to convince us that we aren't talented enough to make art or beautiful enough to be great dancers, we need wise strategies to counteract those negative voices. We need to fight back, so they cannot rob us of the joy of dancing and artmaking.

Recognize the voice of a destructive inner critic: The first step to winning a battle is to see and recognize your enemy. It will be helpful for us to establish a very clear distinction between constructive and destructive criticism, allowing us to quickly differentiate between the two. When destructive self-criticism arises, we need to recognize it right away, so we can take the necessary steps to neutralize its negative influence. When you recognize the voice of a destructive inner critic, **_take a minute pause immediately_**. Take a deep breath and tell yourself that this destructive criticism is damaging your confidence and sabotaging your creative progress. Destructive self-criticism will not do anything to help you become a better dancer or a more creative artist.

Learn to self-accept: We should learn to accept and embrace who we are and what we can do, even though we may not be all perfect. Self-acceptance is ***the very foundation of self-love***, and it is also ***the basis of any healthy self-improvement***. Self-acceptance is a powerful source of positivity that will help us recover our confidence and give us the courage to proudly be our true selves. For example, if your dance classmates can do triple turns and you can only manage a single turn no matter how hard you practice, don't get frustrated. Take time to appreciate the strengths that you do have – perhaps you are great at coming up with new steps or creating new ideas, or maybe you are the popular person whom everyone wants to collaborate with. Pay attention to what you have and be proud of yourself.

Practice self-care: Self-care means taking care of ourselves both mentally and physically. Having sufficient sleep, eating well-balanced meals, and leaving sufficient time in our daily routines to relax and recover are all very important elements of self-care. Our mental states are controlled primarily by our thoughts, but they can also be influenced by the conditions of our physical bodies. For example, dancing while you are "hangry" is not going to help you or anybody around you. When our bodies are hungry or tired, it becomes easy for us to feel anxious and agitated. In this weakened and unstable mental state, we can become vulnerable to our own excessive or destructive criticism. Persistent self-care allows you to have a healthy body and a healthy mind, so you will have enough strength and energy to dance, learn, or do whatever you love.

Surround yourself with positive people: Stopping destructive self-criticism is challenging enough as it is, even without the presence of negative people around us. Other people's comments and behaviors can influence us, whether we like it or not. We should choose the people we want to be around carefully. When you find yourself under the influence of a negative community, remove yourself from that environment as soon as you can. Finding and surrounding yourself with an open-minded and supportive community are some of the best things you can do to help yourself stay positive and strong.

Be generous with self-permission: Be okay with looking silly. Don't be afraid of small failures. Don't let trivial or insignificant risks scare you away before you can test out your cool new ideas. Assess the risks thoughtfully and thoroughly to determine their actual impacts. If it is not something that will hurt other people or yourself, maybe you can ***allow yourself to take a risk***. A completely risk-free life may feel safe in the beginning, but it will become terribly tedious very soon. Embracing risk is an integral part of any creative process, and permitting yourself to take a risk will enable you to take the crucial first step in art, whether it's just to try, play, or purely experience. Without the first step, no artwork will ever be possible.

Work on past traumas: Past traumatic experiences can cause feelings of worthlessness, failure, or guilt, and they can induce the behavior of destructive self-criticism. If you are aware of a past trauma that weighs you down, consider working on it and finding a path to healing for yourself. Talk to an advisor, seek help from a counselor, and consider attending a support group. Actively seek information that can aid in the healing process. Properly addressing and healing from past traumas can significantly contribute to your well-being and help you a long way.

Did you ever have to stop the destructive criticism that you imposed on yourself? What were your best tools or strategies?

____

____

____

____

____

____

____

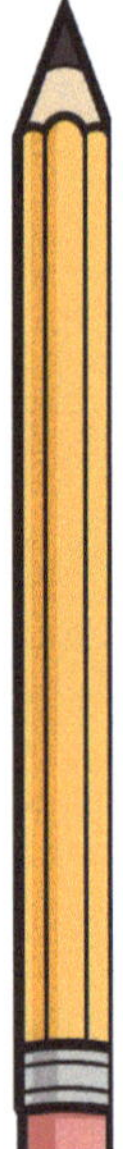

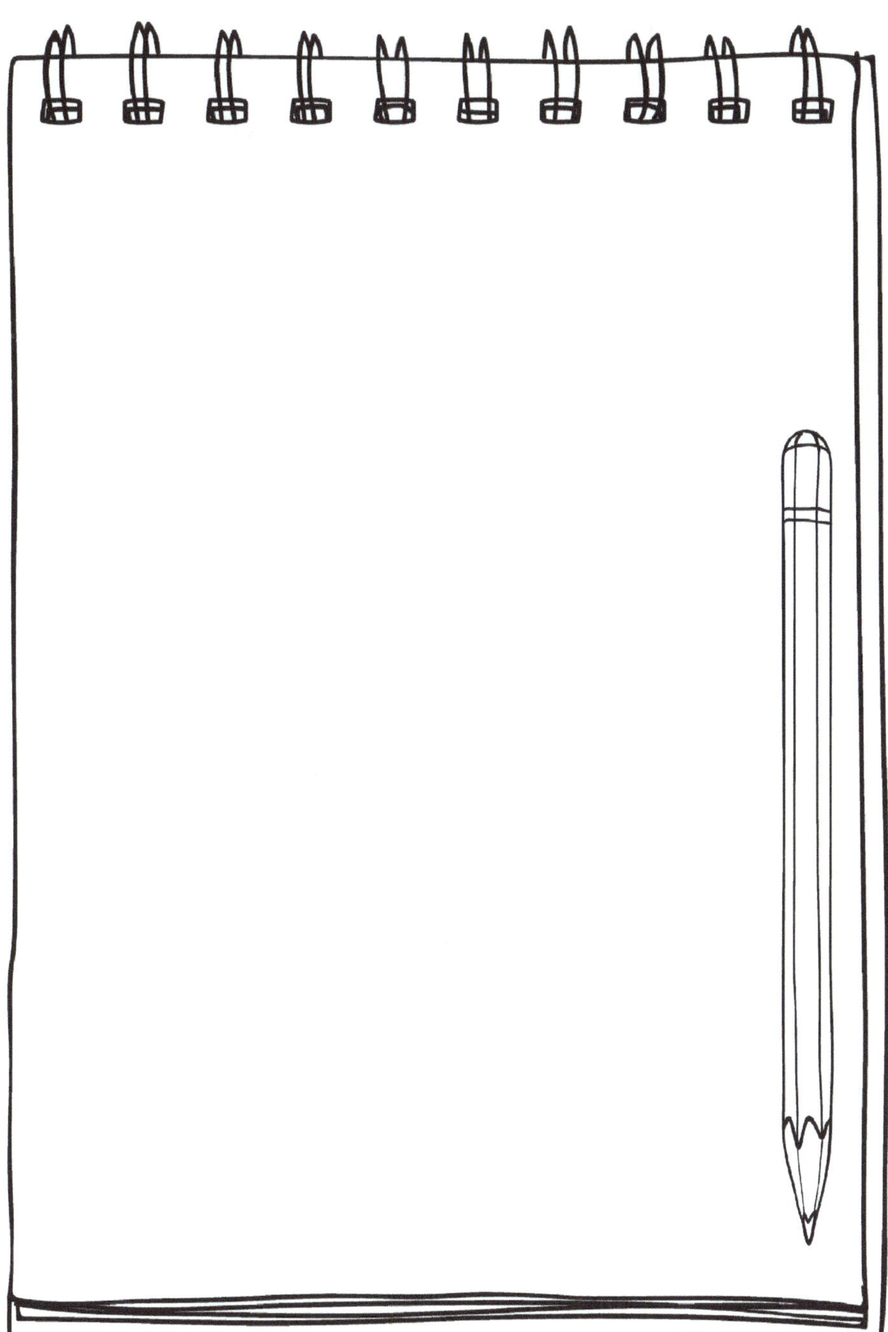

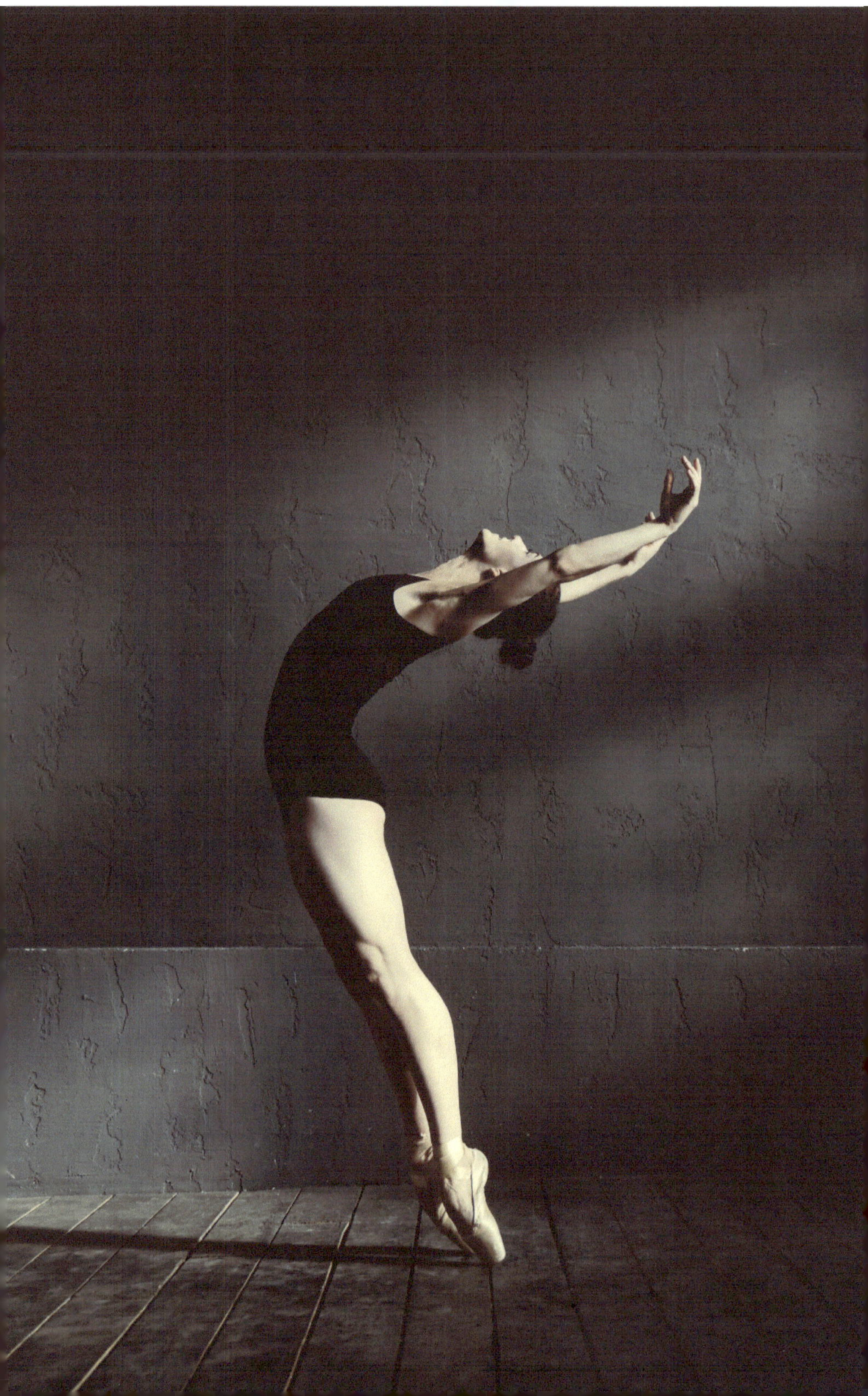

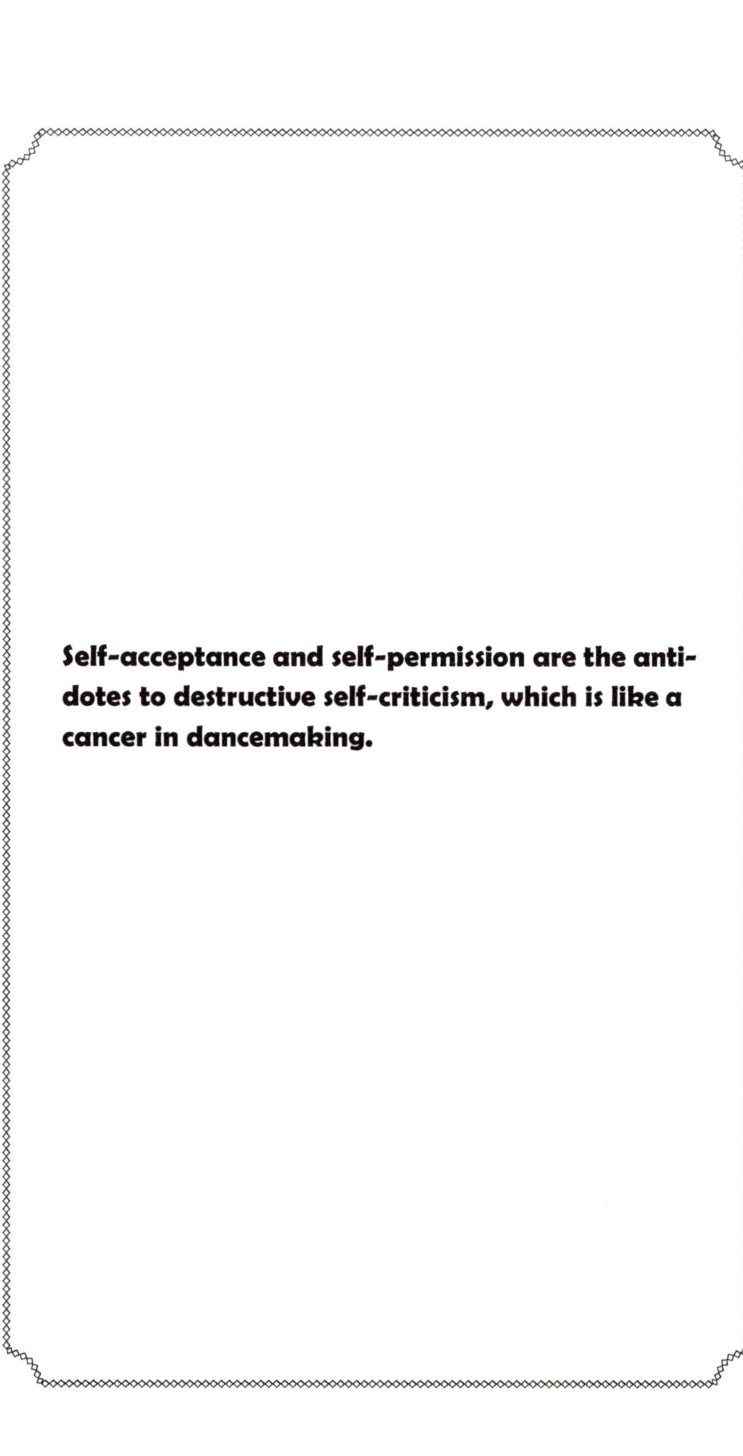

Self-acceptance and self-permission are the anti-dotes to destructive self-criticism, which is like a cancer in dancemaking.

5 Dance To Boost Your Self-confidence

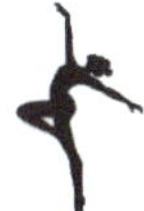

Dancing is among the most effective ways to boost self-confidence. It not only holds great power but is also incredibly enjoyable. When we dance, we must open our hearts to the world and the people around us, whether they are fellow dancers or the audience. We must open ourselves up and be fully present, so the joy of dance can be shared freely with everyone in the room. In the realm of dance, there's no room for self-doubt.

The kind of mental strength that allows us to be confident doesn't come effortlessly. To have this strength and confidence, we will need to work hard for it by practicing regularly. If weight training is something we do to make our physical muscles stronger, dancing can be seen as a type of metaphorical weight training that will strengthen our mental muscles and, thus, boost our self-confidence. What a wonderful way to get our daily doses of mental fitness!

If performing or training in dance can boost one's confidence, how about creating new dances? Creating new dances will require an even higher level of self-confidence. If dancing is the intermediate level of one's confidence training, dancemaking can be seen as the ultimate advanced level of the confidence boot camp.

In a collaborative study with the University of Miami, dance researchers Morejón and Kaminsky discovered that creativity in dance increased the self-esteem and self-confidence of the participating students [7]. It was worth noting that, in the study, the group of students was guided by the instructors to allow moving dialogues based on authentic and aesthetic responses. I would argue that the instructors' facilitation and mutual support among the dance students both played crucial roles. In this facilitated creative environment, students were guided away from excessive or destructive self-criticism, a tendency known to erode one's self-confidence and self-esteem (see "Chapter 4" for more details about avoiding destructive self-criticism). By reducing the tendency of excessive or destructive self-criticism, the participating students were able to find joy and empowerment in the process of dancemaking.

When we make a new dance, no one will tell us what steps we should choose or what ideas we should follow. There are no set rules in creativity and no answers that are right or wrong. Sometimes, creating a new dance may feel like walking on a vast open meadowland or sailing in an open ocean without a compass. You don't know if you are going in the right direction or how much longer it will take to arrive at your destination. The only thing you can do is trust yourself, trust your intuition and **just keep going**. You are the captain to steer your creative process. To do these things, you will need a very strong sense of self-trust and self-confidence.

You may be wondering, once a dance is created, can the artist finally take a break? I wish I could say "Yes," but sometimes dance-making can be an enormously difficult endeavor. Normally, upon completion of a job, we expect a reasonable and fair reward. When you study at school, your teacher may praise you for a well-written research paper. When you work in a job, your boss may offer you a raise or a promotion in recognition of your contributions to the business. However, the reward system doesn't always work like that in the world of art.

We should remember that some of the greatest artists in history were never adequately recognized or rewarded for their contributions during their lifetimes. Vincent van Gogh is widely regarded as one of the greatest Dutch painters and post-impressionists. During the time he created his paintings, van Gogh did not achieve recognition as a successful painter. Although he created 800 oil paintings and 700 drawings, he had only ever sold one piece of art in his lifetime and was always desperately poor [8]. Throughout his life, van Gogh never received the recognition or respect he deserved.

Another pointed example is *The Rite of Spring*, which stands as one of the most influential modern ballets of the 20th century. The ballet music was composed by Igor Stravinsky and commissioned by the famous founder of Ballets Russes, Serge Diaghilev [9]. When *The Rite of Spring* premiered in Paris in 1913, it almost caused a scandal. The audience was greatly offended by the unconventional music and choreography of the new ballet. During the performance, the angry audience grew into an uproar and shouted at the musicians on stage; the audience was so loud that the dancers were unable to hear their music cues from the orchestra pit. In her autobiography, Polish-born English dancer and pedagogue Marie Rambert noted that the audience was, in fact, offended by the choreography itself, "as dancers mimicked movements that seemed to require some kind of medical attention [10]." That was how the audience in Paris reacted to the great ballet over a century ago!

While we strive to share our art with as many people as possible, it is never guaranteed that the audience will love our new dances. After months or years of grueling studio practice, choreography, and rehearsals, it is not even guaranteed that there will be enough audience to fill the seats in a dance recital. This is the harsh reality. However, despite all possible frustration, you must continue to **believe in yourself and work hard on your art**. Preserve your self-confidence and composure, so you can continue to confront challenges and carry on the tasks in your creative journey, regardless of the outcomes.

It may not be an easy journey, but if you possess the confidence and courage to continue dancing and creating new dance works, you will find the strength to be the fiercest fighter in the challenges of life.

7 Morejón, J.L. (2021)

8 Editors of Encyclopaedia Britannica (2023, March 26)

9 Schwarm, B. (2023, April 16)

10 Rambert, M. (1972)

Dance Notes ~ write down your thoughts!

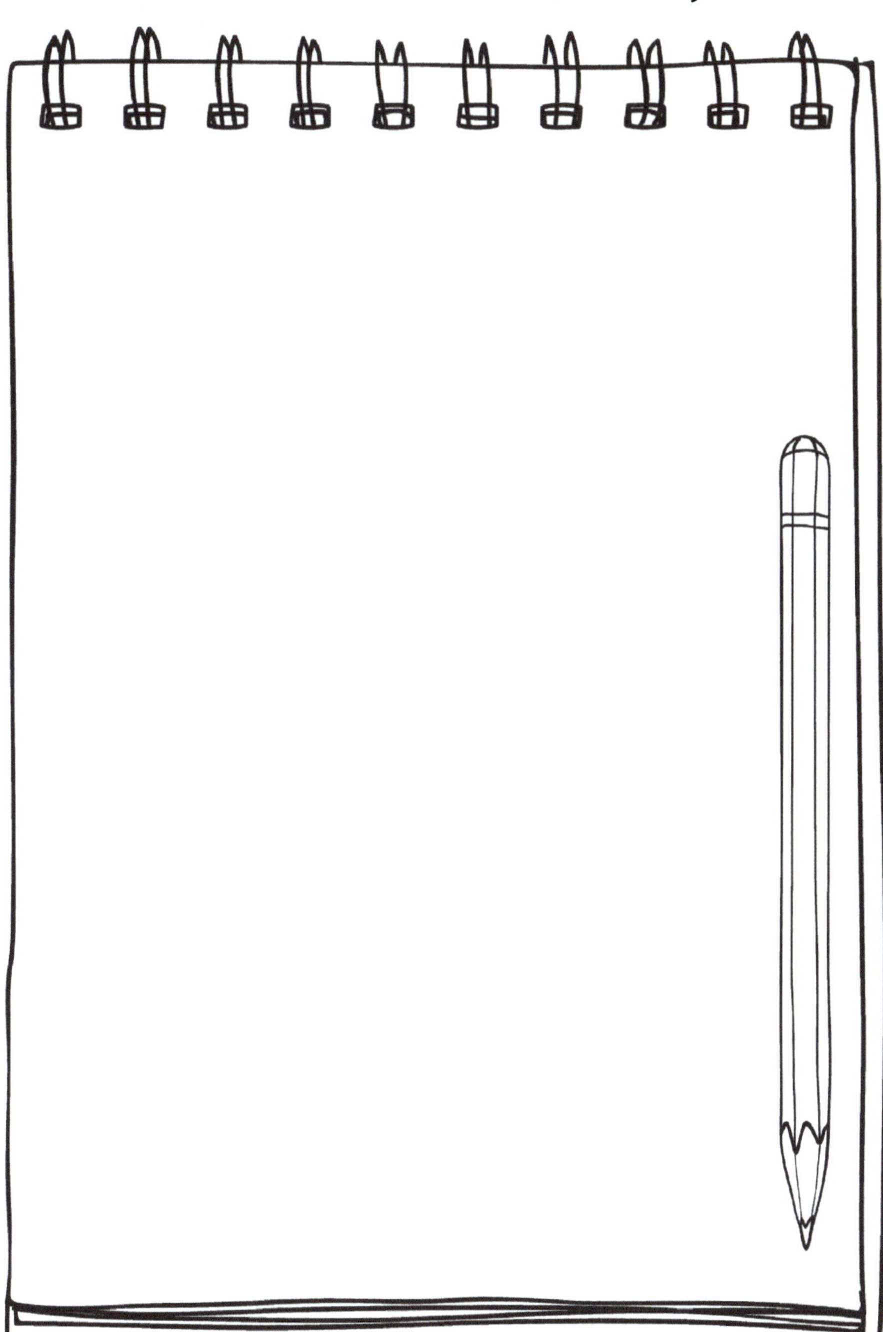

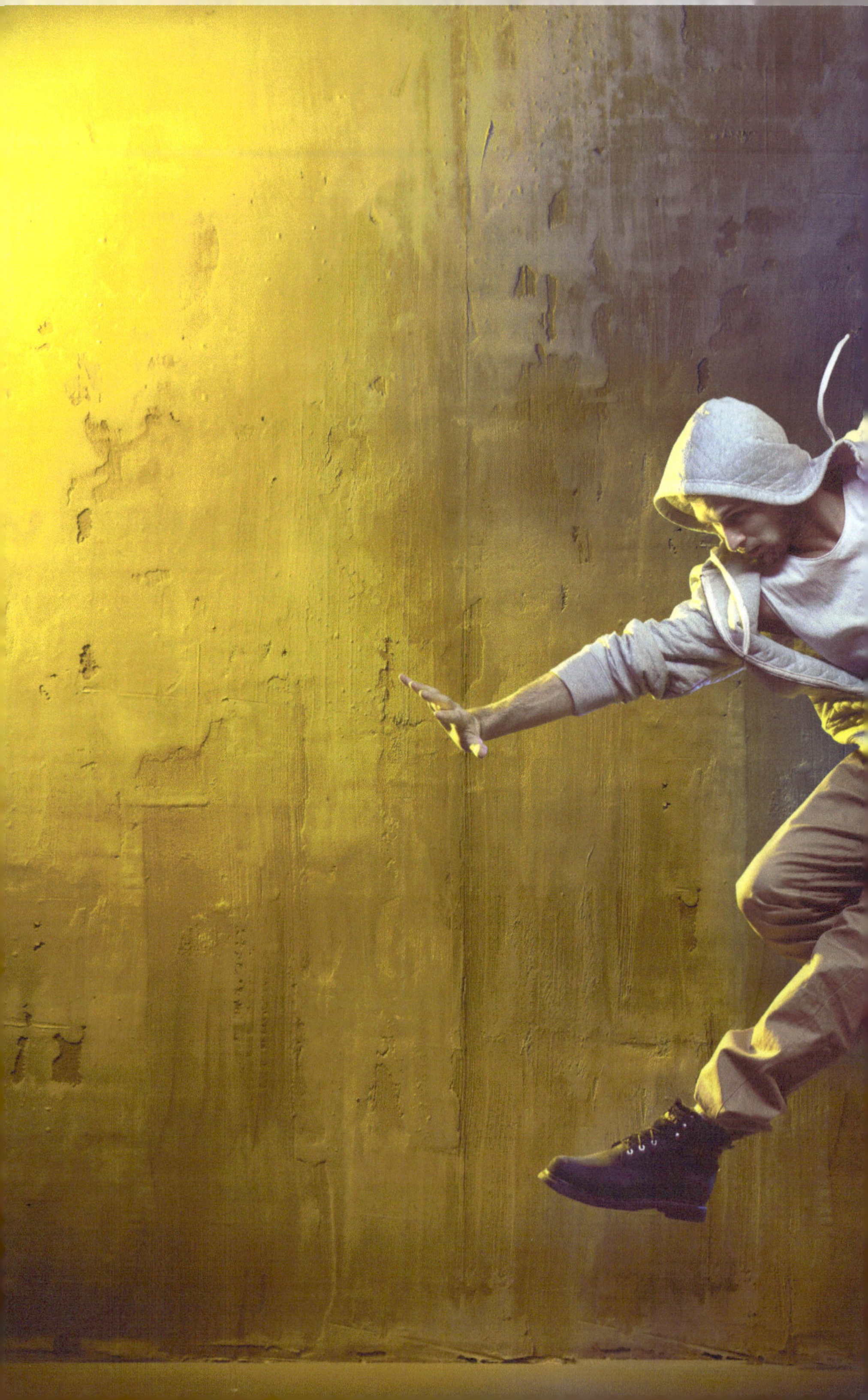

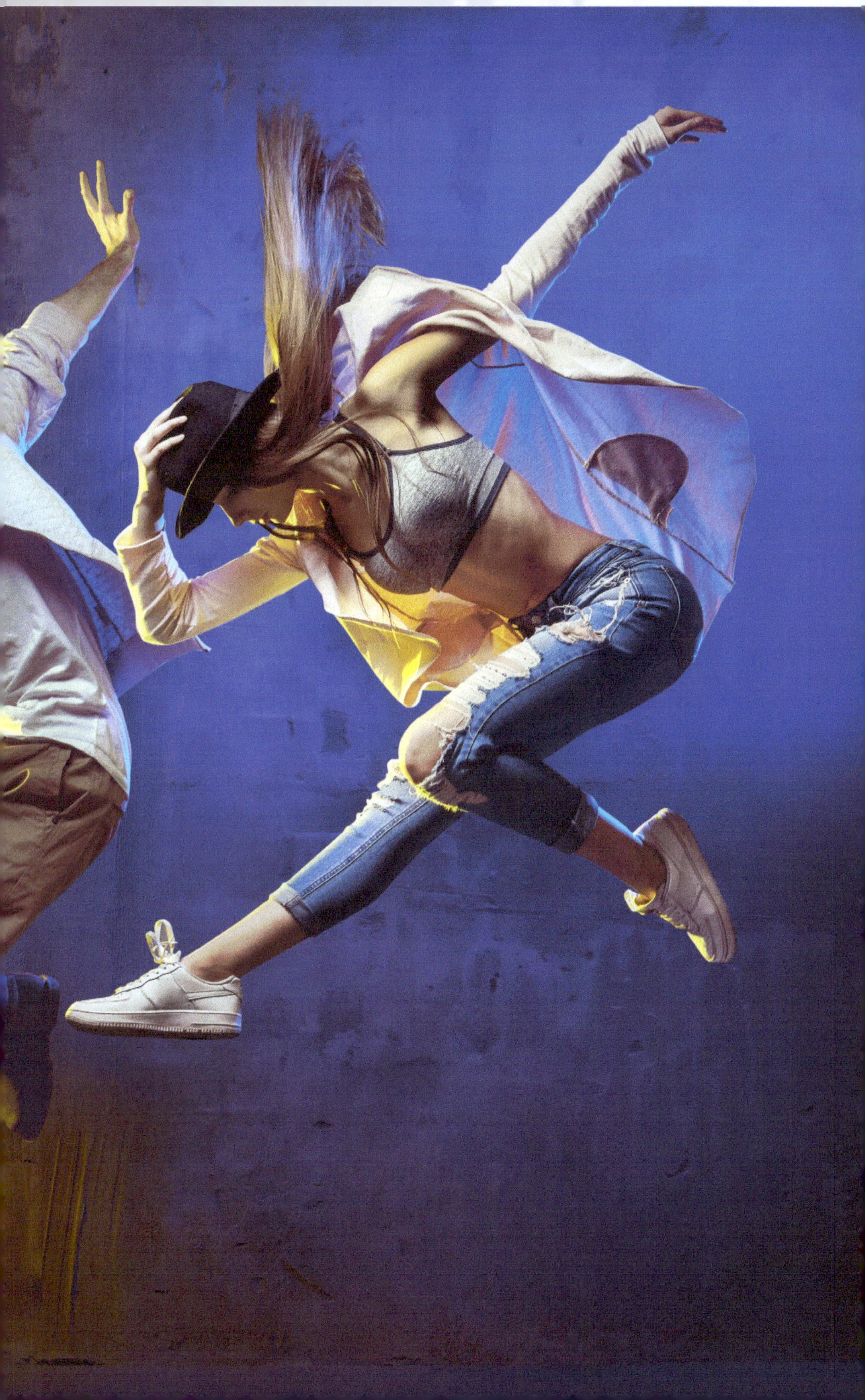

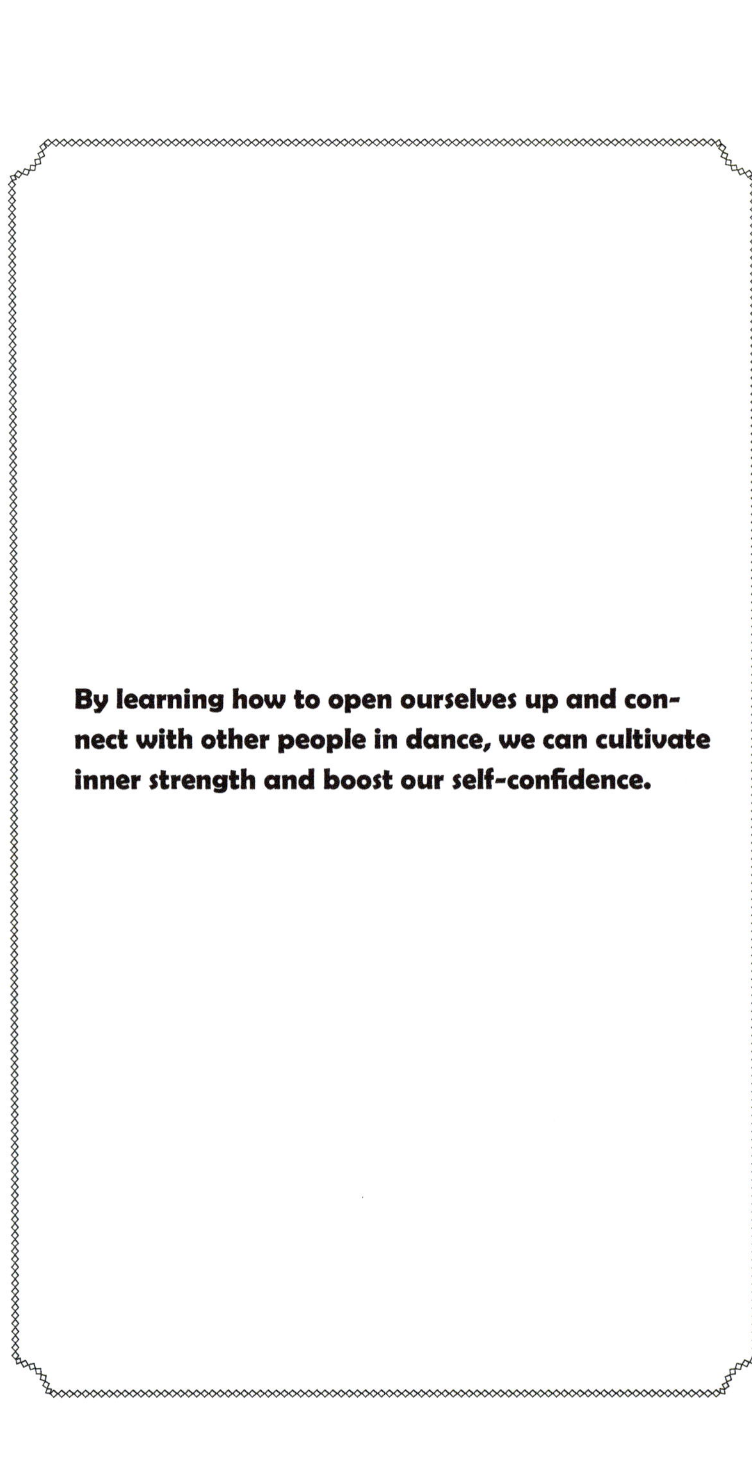

By learning how to open ourselves up and connect with other people in dance, we can cultivate inner strength and boost our self-confidence.

6 Keep An Open Mind

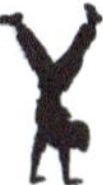

Artmaking depends largely on our ability to think creatively and to innovate. According to Anna Powers, an award-winning scientist, a person's open-mindedness can directly increase their imagination and creativity [11]. Open-mindedness is a trait that allows a person to **consider various ideas, even when those ideas may contradict one's initial belief**. With open-mindedness, a person will be able to look at different sources of information, and by doing so, find the truth through continuous research and questioning. As dance artists, it is no surprise that we should keep open-mindedness at the top of our priority list, so it can help us expand our experiences and enhance our creativity.

Aside from enhancing our creativity, keeping an open mind can help us become more insightful. It will help us develop the ability to deal with ambiguous situations and enhance our reasoning skills.

In a psychological study done by researchers Fujita, Gollwitzer and Oettingen, it has been proven that open-mindedness can make a person think smarter in an ambiguous situation, both consciously and subconsciously [12]. When you have an open mind, you can more easily access the memory of information that appears to be "incidental" to the ongoing task. With this open mindset, you will also get better at selecting important information that contributes to achieving your goals.

Has being open-minded ever helped you identify more potential solutions in a challenging situation? Please reflect on your experience.

Dance is an art that requires open-mindedness as dancemaking thrives in new possibilities. While it may seem surprising, staying open-minded can sometimes be a challenge in dance. Why? There are numerous reasons, but one that significantly affects young dancers is the formation of tight-knit social circles or cliques within dance schools and dance communities. When small circles or cliques form in a dance community, social expectations or peer pressure may hinder our ability to keep an open mind, preventing us from considering *a broad range of diverse values or voices*.

Most dance students would take classes at their favorite dance schools. There is nothing wrong with that. It is completely understandable and natural that we want to be around people whom we feel familiar with and trust. Sticking with the same teachers can help us explore dance movements on a deeper and more nuanced level because our bodies are already familiar with the movement style or technique. Teachers who have known us personally and are aware of our training history can give us the type of support that a new teacher may not be able to provide. Meanwhile, developing close friendships at a dance school is a highly enjoyable experience and a crucial factor in the learning process, particularly for many young dancers.

However, when we limit our exposure to the same small group of people over a long period without sufficient exposure to outside voices, it becomes easy for us to grow accustomed to the same set of values and beliefs. Gradually, we may fall into the trap of confirmation bias. You don't need to be a narrow-minded or unintelligent person to hold confirmation bias; it is just part of our human nature that has long existed in the evolution of mankind.

Confirmation bias is a tendency for one to favor only the information that is consistent with one's existing beliefs and discount information that is not. We often see people from opposite political spectrums struggle to reach any consensus in a debate; confirmation bias may be a contributing factor preventing mutual understanding. In his 2022 publication, Peters explained that confirmation bias existed in human evolution to prevent people from being epistemically disconnected from their groups. In other words, this behavior pattern has existed to ensure that people in the same societal group will hold the same point of view, so they get better chances of success or survival by collaborating toward common goals [13]. However, with confirmation bias, it becomes very easy for us to *falsely reject information that is true but may not support our current expectations*. It will prevent us from keeping an open mind to any different or dissenting voices.

Even though there is a strong appeal in sticking with our favorite people in dance, the lack of exposure to different dance styles and teachings can lead to the development of tunnel vision. It is less common for dance students to discreetly split their time taking classes at different dance schools that uphold different values or give different styles of dance teaching. To prevent tunnel vision or confirmation bias, we will need to make a conscious effort to **listen to different voices from various people and communities**. This is the extra work we need to do to maintain our open-mindedness.

The dance world is wonderful in a way that there are many live performances. When we attend a dance concert, we have a perfect opportunity to meet different people before or after a performance. Don't hang out only with the people you already know. Try talking to the people sitting next to you, even if they are strangers. Oftentimes, strangers can bring us remarkably intelligent insights, drawing from their diverse backgrounds. When you can, stay for a post-performance event and listen to what the artists have to say. Don't be afraid to raise your hand and ask questions in a Q&A. What you hear may amaze you and give you a refreshing new perspective for your dance practice.

There are many different ways to explore new ideas and new communities. The best way to understand other people's thinking is to be proactive and reach out to them. Most people won't hesitate to give you their best answers when approached respectfully. In fact, they may even feel flattered that you are seeking to understand their opinions. If there is something people have said that baffles you or contradicts your current beliefs, consider checking out your local libraries. Books can help us to understand a subject matter on a deeper level and provide broader, more comprehensive points of view.

The Internet can also serve as a great source of information with proper fact-checking. When surfing the Internet, try to go with information from reliable sources, such as government or university websites where information is verified and based on science. Take what you read on social media with a grain of salt. Some algorithms on these social platforms tend to bias the objectivity of information based on a user's browsing history. They will provide you with information anticipated to match your interests, aiming to keep you interested in their platforms for longer. In any controversial discussion, listen to comments from both sides of the debate and make an effort to understand every perspective using your reasoning skills and empathy.

When you keep an open mind, you have a much better chance to make well-informed decisions for yourself, your art, and your career. You will be able to listen to diverse voices, understand people's opinions from different angles, and empathize with those around you. These qualities will contribute to establishing a harmonious and genuine social network, which will, in return, provide you with the support to maintain your open mindset. What's more – your beliefs and opinions will inevitably be reflected in your art. With an open and empathetic heart, your art will gain the power to resonate with a broader and more diverse audience, bringing more positivity, hope, and healing into the world.

Attending live events is a great way to meet new people and maintain our open mindset. How many times have you done the following in the past year?

- [ ] Attend a live concert

- [ ] Take a dance workshop or master class from a local or touring artist

- [ ] In a dance concert, talk to a stranger sitting next to you

- [ ] Before or after a dance concert, attend a Q&A to understand the artist's creative process

- [ ] Engage in conversation with people from diverse backgrounds

- [ ] On a dance-related controversial topic, conduct research in a library

11 Powers, A. (2018, December 7)

12 Fujita, K., Gollwitzer, P.M., and Oettingen, G. (2007, January)

13 Peters, U (2022)

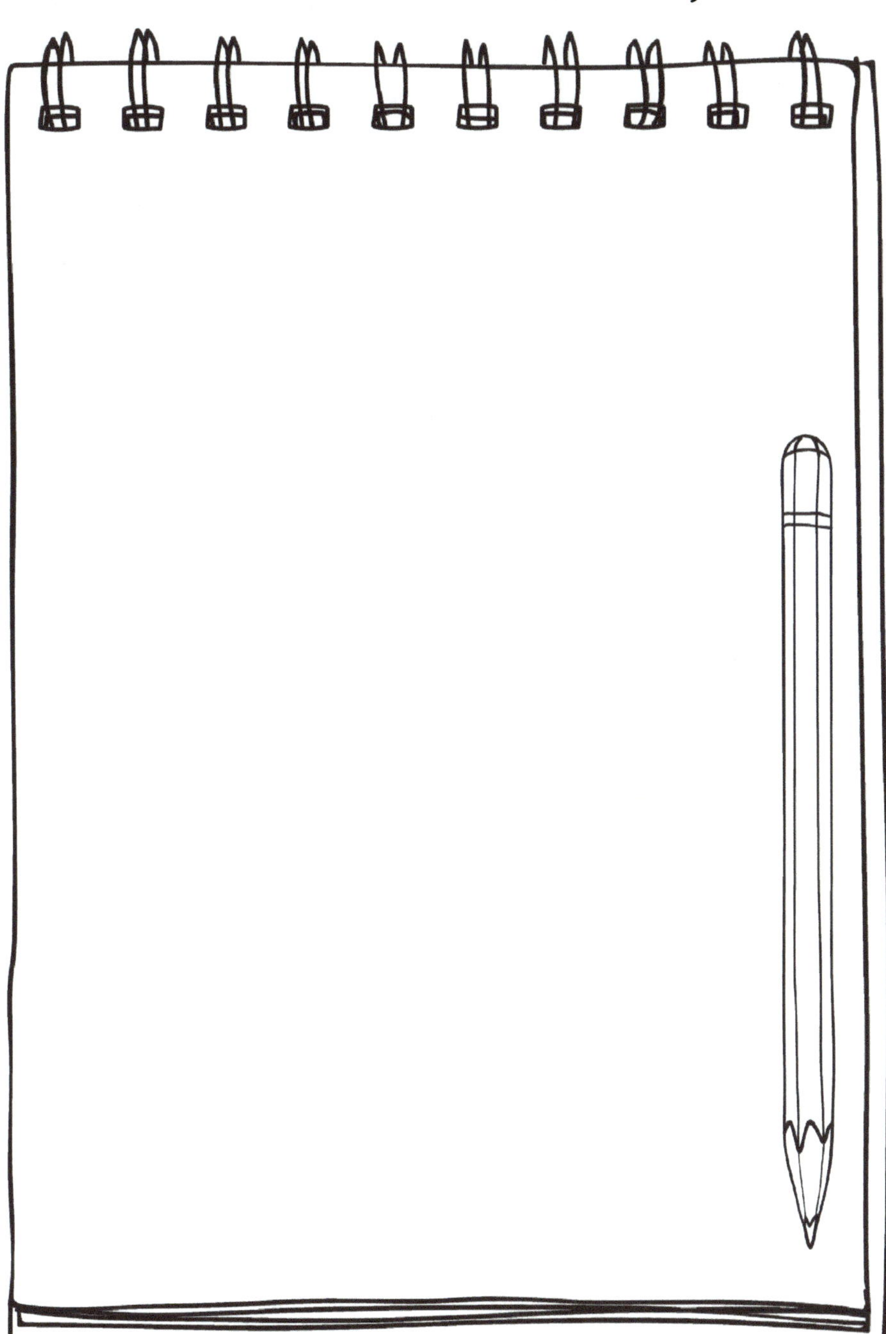

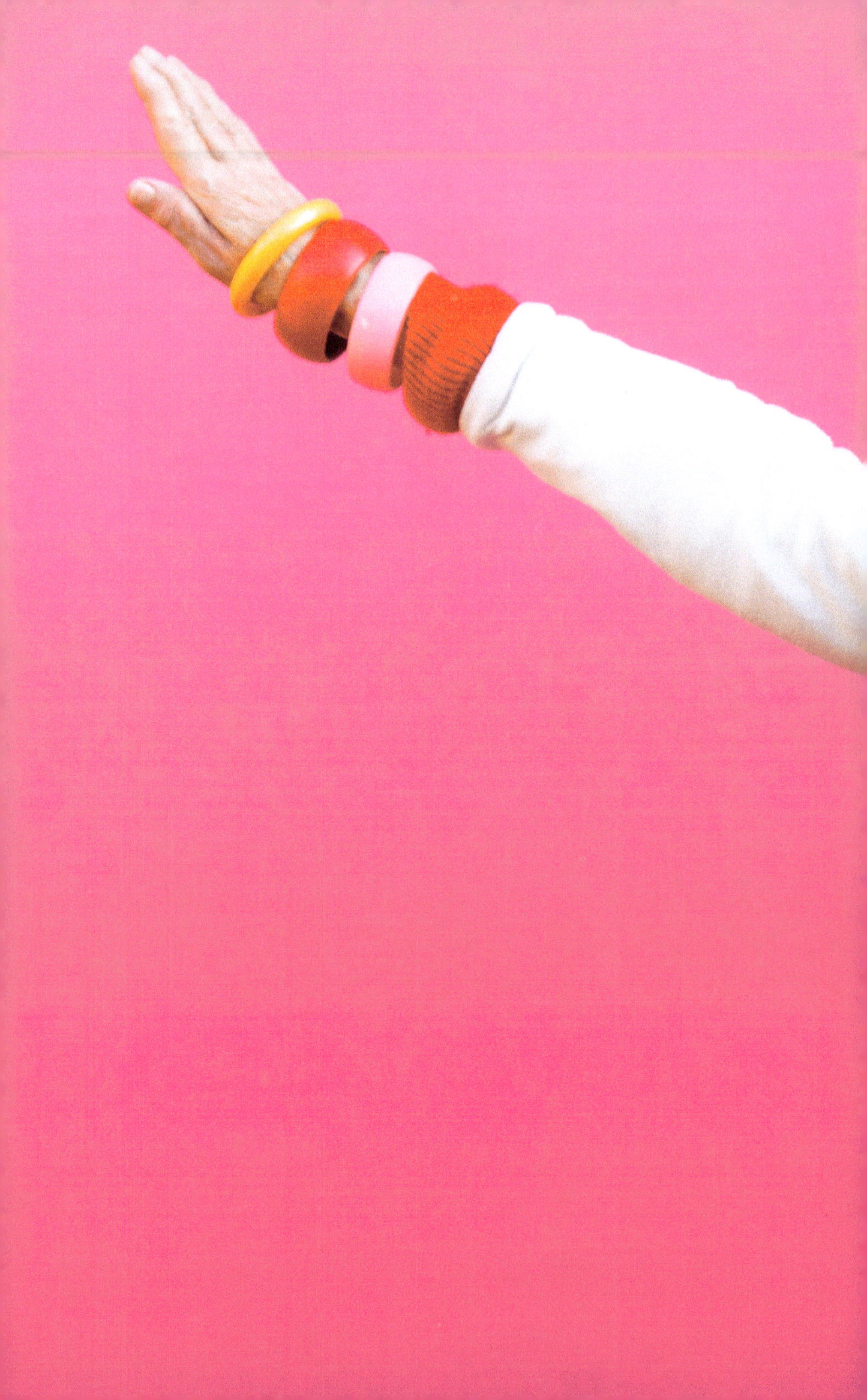

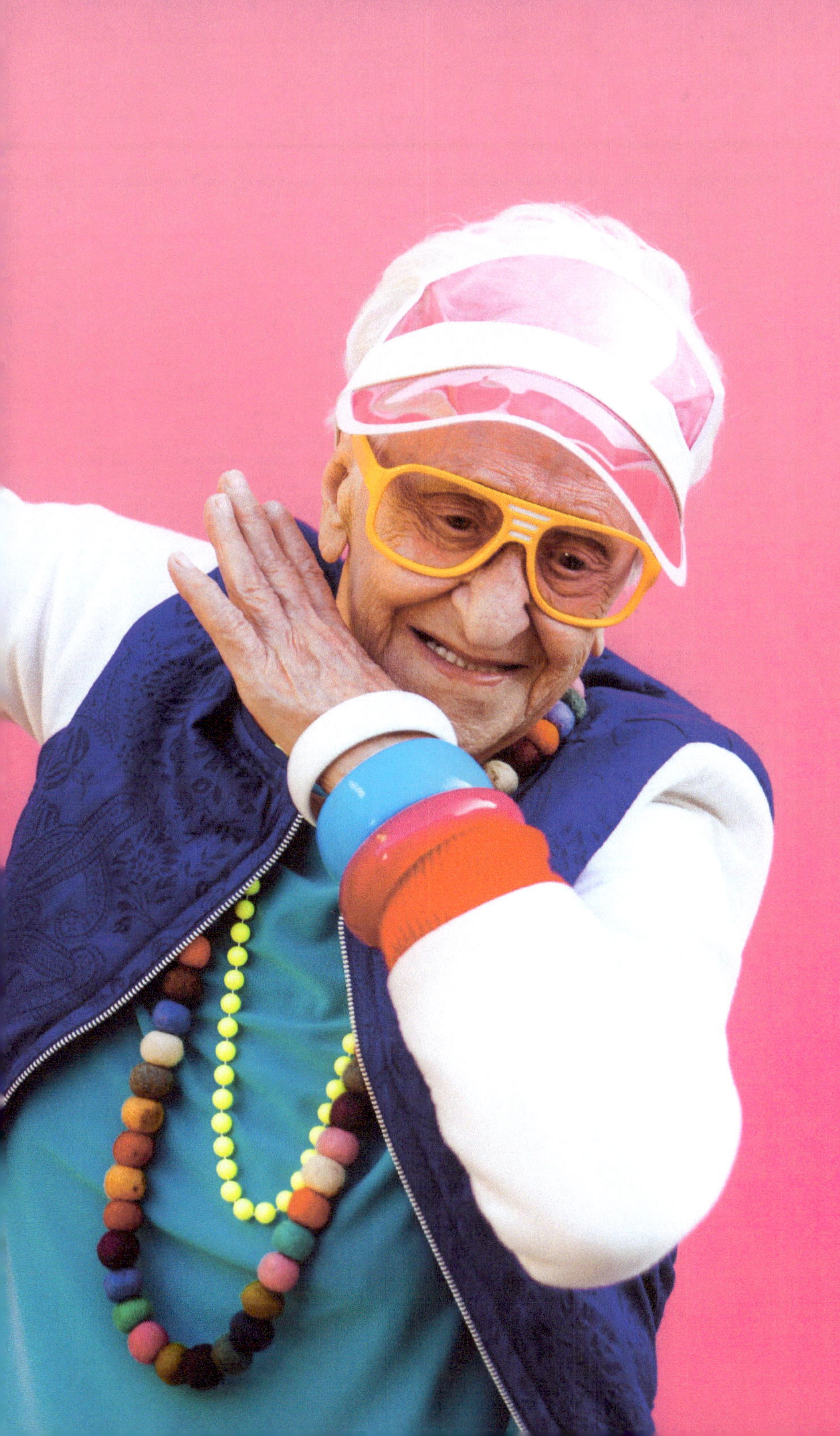

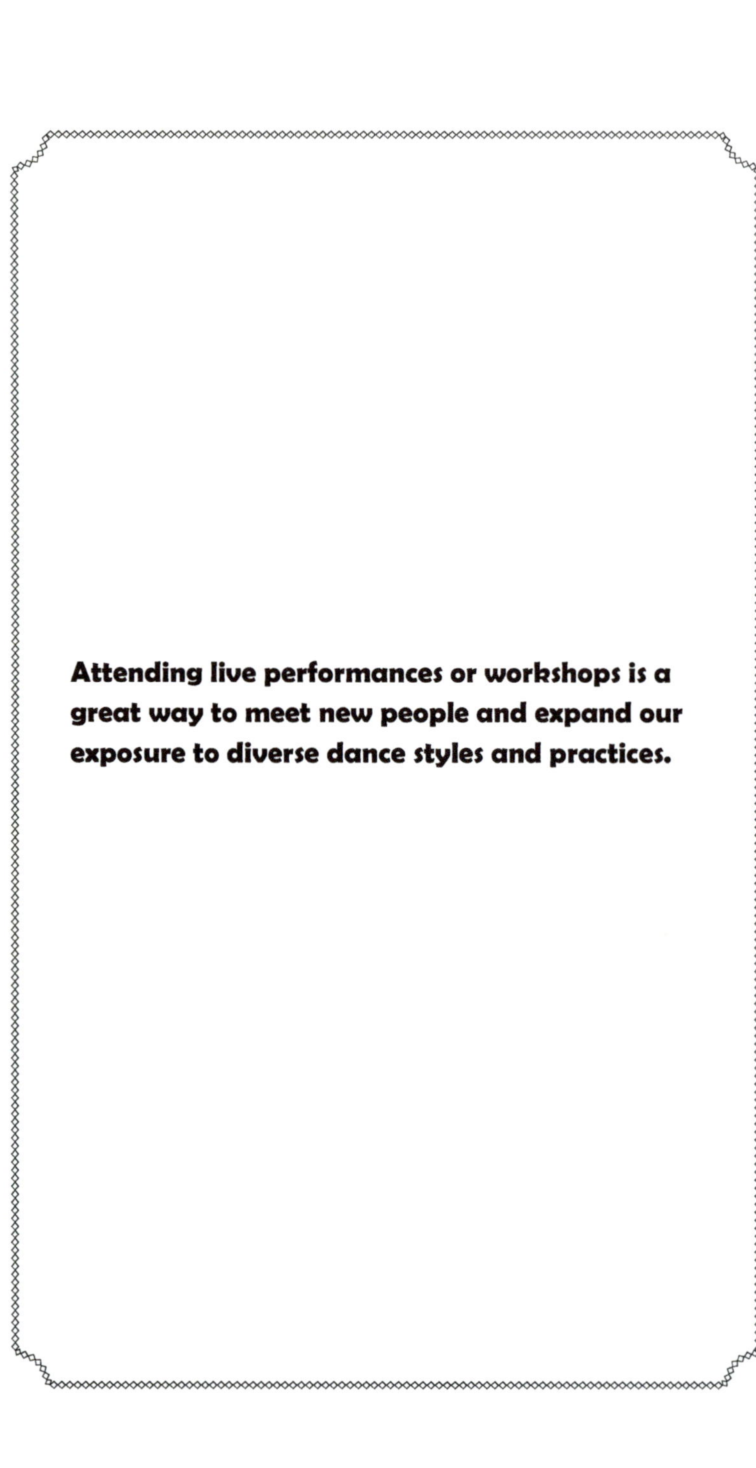

Attending live performances or workshops is a great way to meet new people and expand our exposure to diverse dance styles and practices.

7 Having Diverse Skills Can Help You Succeed

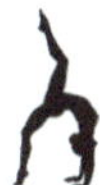

Although traditional dance education often encourages dancers to devote most of their time to the perfection of dance techniques, focusing excessively on just one or two skills may not be the most effective way to prepare young and aspiring dancers for today's fast-evolving world. Skills such as visual design, communication, computer fluency, collaboration, research, and critical thinking should also be considered seriously.

The notion that "a professional dancer only needs to know dance" is obsolete. Nowadays, having diverse skills can greatly empower dance artists. The dance field is competitive and challenging, and resources for dancers are often limited. It is very common for dancers to encounter bottlenecks when pursuing their careers. Being multi-skilled can enhance one's ability to ***think outside the box*** and

creatively solve problems. When facing obstacles in your dance or personal life, the ability to think outside the box can create more opportunities, thereby increasing your chances of success.

There are more types of skill sets out there than you and I can know of. When choosing the skills that you want to learn, there is no wrong way to go about it. Feel free to choose any skills that interest you or spark your excitement to learn, even those not directly related to dance. You have the flexibility to explore a diverse range of skills that align with your interests and aspirations. In dance, there are important skills that are frequently in demand. Some familiar examples are:

- » Choreography
- » Costume design
- » Stage design
- » Writing
- » Public speaking
- » Event and project management
- » Fundraising and publicity
- » Multilingual skills (Google and AI translation apps are great tools, but learning another language can give you a deeper understanding of other people's cultures)

You may be wondering, "How can these additional skills help a dancer succeed?" Having a range of skills can help you pursue diverse interests and expand your social connections; you may also get opportunities to transfer some of your expertise from one job to the next. It's like giving yourself an extra boost to extend your career trajectory. Having these additional skills will give you more options in your career at every turn, making you a more desirable candidate for a potential employer or client under certain circumstances.

For example, being a dancer with costume design skills can come in very handy for yourself or your dance group. If your dance group doesn't have a professional costume designer, you can help fellow dancers come up with cool costume ideas before an important dance event. Even if there is already a professional costume designer in the company, you can be the second pair of eyes and share your feedback with the designer. Your understanding of both the dance and costume design will render you an excellent communicator in both fields. Nothing is better for a costume designer than to receive direct feedback from a dancer who can communicate clearly and effectively.

If you are a dancer with strong written communication skills, you can become the go-to person whom everybody asks for help. Many dance artists do not find joy in paperwork and writing; this is a drawback, not a strength! If your dance director is overwhelmed with writing a press release or grant application, your offer to help edit or complete these tasks will certainly be appreciated. When you do this, you can learn more about the dance company from a business perspective. It may give you some interesting ideas on how to organize your own dance group in the future. If you enjoy writing and have extra time besides your routine dance rehearsals, consider negotiating with the company to take on a side job as a grant writer. There is nothing wrong with earning some additional income! The exhilarating aspect of possessing a versatile skill set is that ***each opportunity tends to pave the way for the next***, and you will never know what the ultimate outcome might be, making it an unpredictable and thrilling journey.

If you are a dancer with excellent public speaking or storytelling abilities, you may become the voice for your dance company. A post-performance Q&A session is a good example – when you're adept at public speaking and quick thinking, you can give the most sincere and in-depth answer to an audience's question during a Q&A session. Audiences love to hear directly from the dancers. Another example is artist interviews. If you're comfortable with public speaking, you can engage in public interviews with the press or host a podcast. Conducting public interviews will provide your dance organization with increased public exposure. In doing so, you can assist your dance company in establishing stronger connections with the community, reaching new audiences, and attracting potential sponsors.

If you are a choreographer looking for opportunities to develop new pieces or stage your existing dances, having diverse skills will certainly help you. You'll find more opportunities if you can choreograph for both dance stages and dance videos. Due to the inherently limited number of theaters in a city, only a small percentage of choreographers and artists will get the chance to present their works in major theaters. However, the opportunities to produce dance videos are far less restricted.

Dance videos can be kept and watched for years once they are made, and they can be watched by people around the world with minimal geographic restrictions. You possess the ability to reach out to every person on this planet who has access to the internet and is interested in experiencing your art! Today, the technological advancement of cameras and video-editing software has made it so much easier for artists to create dance videos on limited budgets. If you know how to leverage the right technology for your art, you can break barriers and share your dance with the world. It will embody Walt Disney's famous quote, "If you can dream it, you can do it."

Having diverse skills will enhance your **interdisciplinary thinking**. Not only will it give you more opportunities in your career, but it will also make you more intelligent and innovative. Dr. Kabir Sehgal, a Grammy-winning producer, composer, bestselling author, navy officer, investment banker, and corporate strategist, exemplifies this type of multi-dimensional intelligence and an extensive array of talents. In a Harvard Business Review article, Sehgal explained that when you are good at different jobs, you can identify where *the best ideas from each discipline should interact* [14]. Your understanding of one area will support and stimulate your creativity in another. Instead of remaining isolated in their separate corners, your knowledge and skills in each discipline will interact, collide, fuse, and contribute to your holistic growth.

When you invest your time and energy in cultivating a diverse set of skills, the process of continuous learning and interdisciplinary thinking may inspire you to come up with the next revolutionary idea in dance. All you need to do is follow your curiosity and passion, allowing yourself to come up with *creative and unconventional ideas!* As Sehgal claimed, "By doing more than one job, you may end up doing all of them better." When you have diverse skills and the ability for interdisciplinary thinking, the increased benefits won't just add up – they will compound. The endless possibilities can lead you to places you might have never expected when you first started.

---

14 Sehgal, K. (2017, April 25)

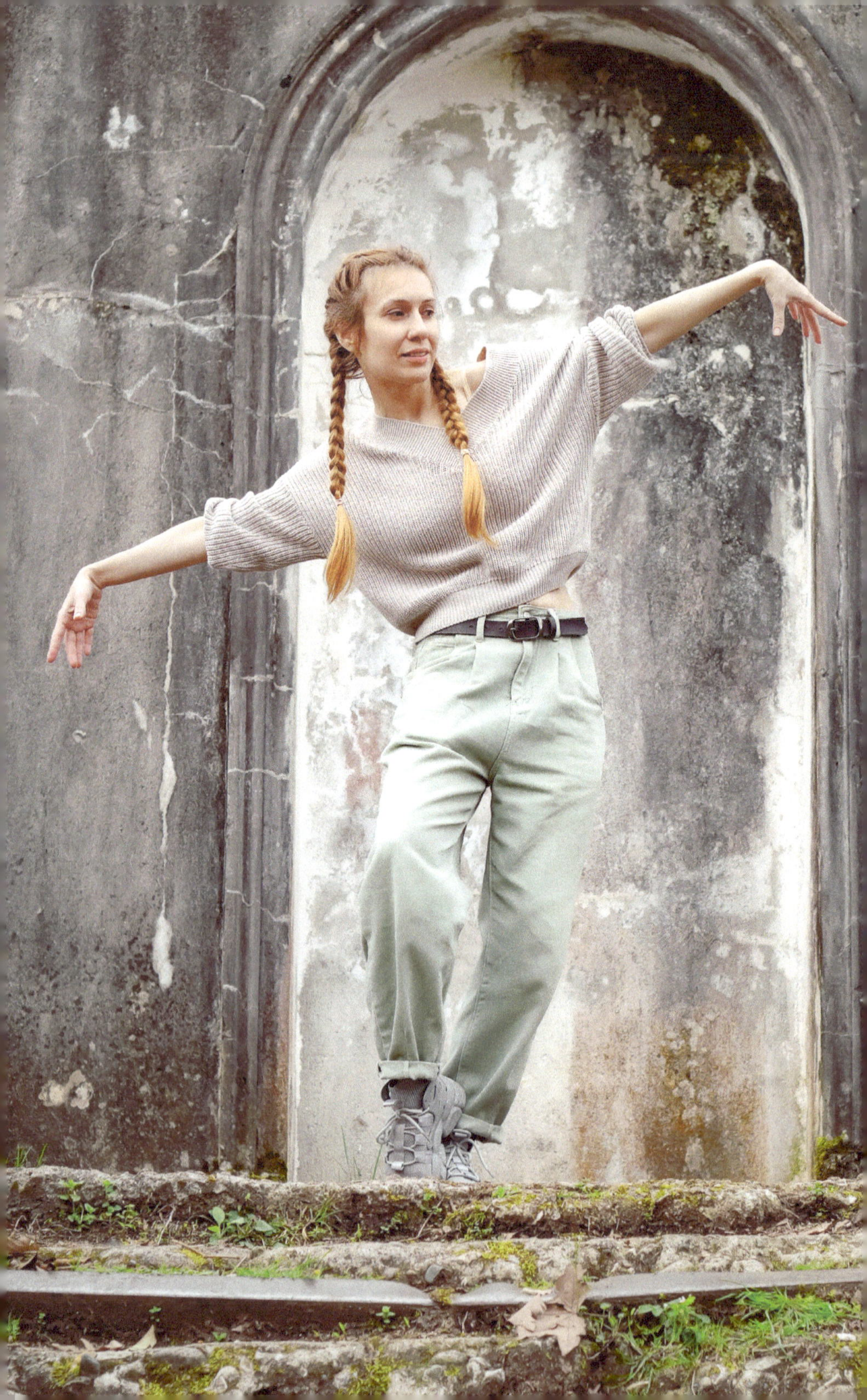

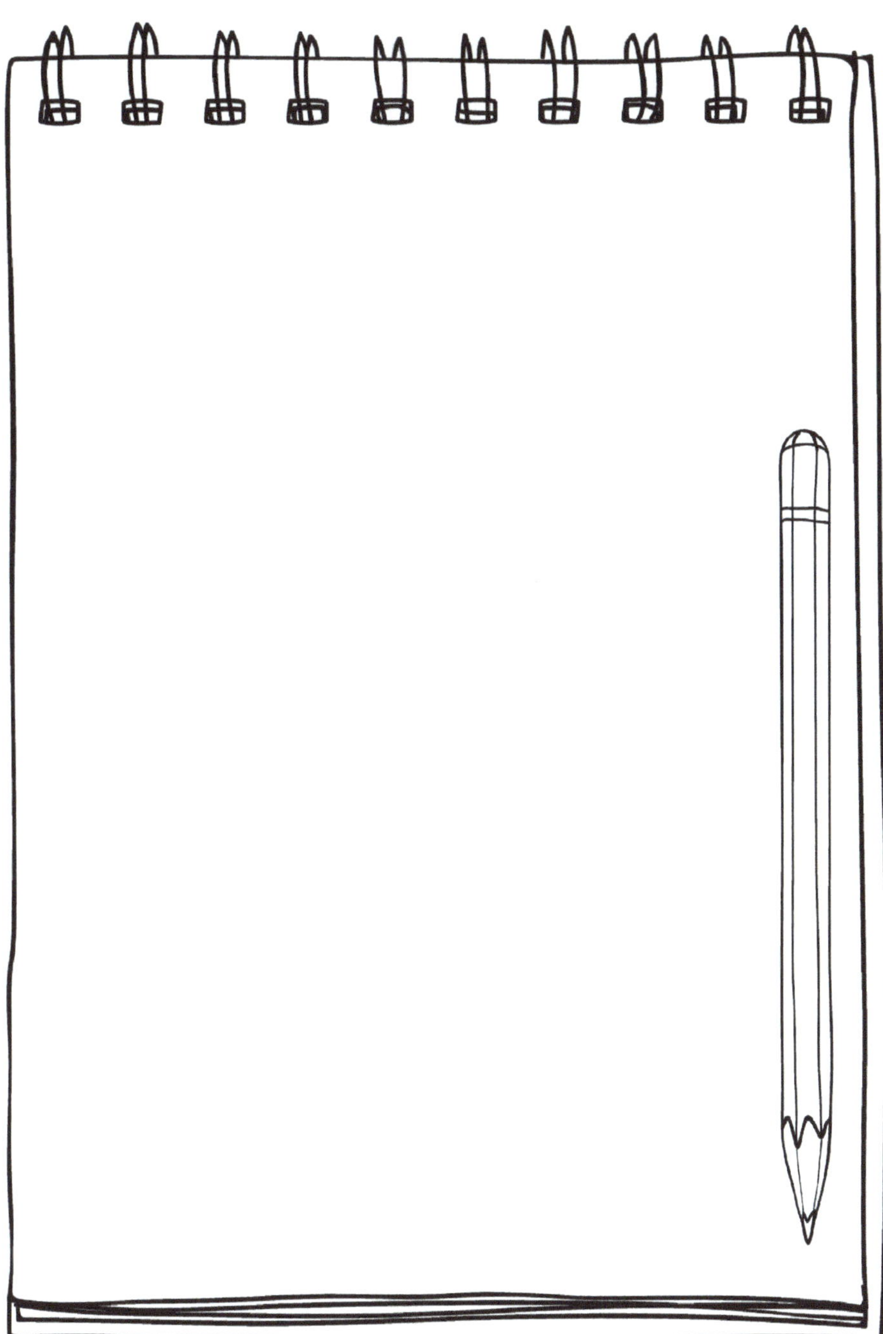

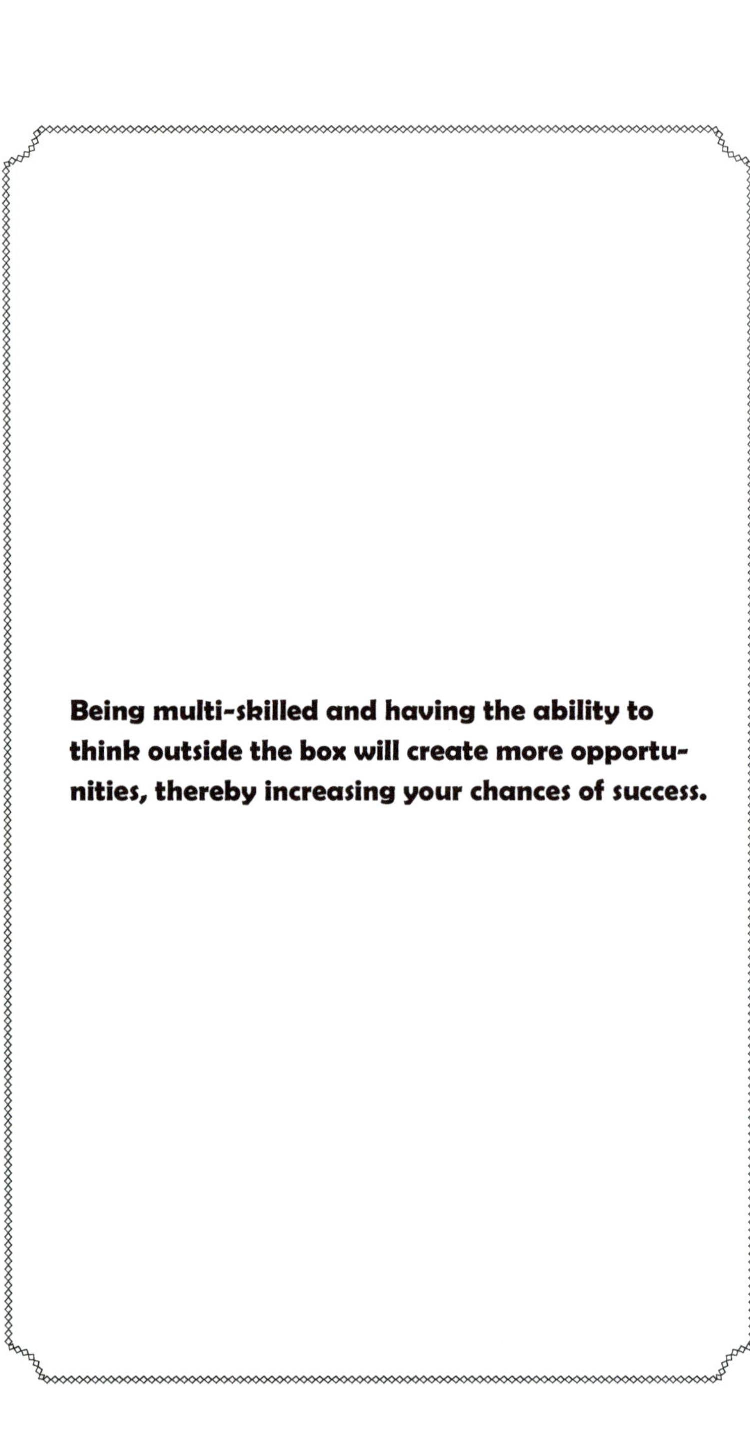
Being multi-skilled and having the ability to think outside the box will create more opportunities, thereby increasing your chances of success.

8 Establish Your Own Learning Schedule

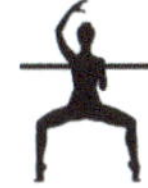

Dancers should appreciate the importance of discipline and consistency better than people in any other field. Discipline and consistency are the cornerstones of dance training. Many dance schools provide class schedules for dancers to adhere to as part of their regular practice. These schedules are essential to dancers' training; they are what allow dancers to establish consistent routines and build momentum to improve their dance skills on a daily or weekly basis.

However, to transform into versatile dance artists equipped with diverse skills, interdisciplinary creativity (refer to Section 7), and readiness for the future, we need to broaden our focus beyond solely relying on traditional dance techniques. Dance techniques are important, but they are not the only skills you will need to succeed as a dancer and have a good life in this world. In addition to dance classes and rehearsals, perhaps we want to explore subjects related to choreography, stage design, creative writing, communication, computer fluency, and even business entrepreneurship.

To achieve this, we will need learning schedules that can facilitate the consistent development of these additional skills. "Practice makes perfect" – this saying applies to dance just as it does to other disciplines. To excel in any pursuit, we must invest time and effort in practice and learning.

Consider establishing your learning schedule to practice one or more of the following skills regularly. Feel free to add any additional skills that pique your interest. Indicate the number of times you commit to practicing each week.

- [ ] Practice choreography or improvisation

- [ ] Engage in creative writing

- [ ] Play a musical instrument

- [ ] Learn stage design (costume design, light design, sound design, etc.)

____

____

It may feel like a lot of work in the beginning. Many dancers excel at following schedules provided by their instructors. However, it will take a completely different set of mental muscles to **establish your own learning schedule and stick to it**. The process will require a considerable amount of determination and willpower. Nonetheless, if you recognize that these skills may one day be the keys to your success in life or as an artist, you will understand that the time and effort you invest today will be worthwhile. These additional tasks may add to the workload of your already busy daily schedule, but your efforts will eventually yield positive results.

Successfully planning and executing your learning schedule undoubtedly requires self-discipline. If you haven't had many opportunities to do so, you'll discover numerous side benefits in the process of establishing your learning schedule:

◊   You get to choose and define your own goals and creative visions.

◊   The ability to create plans and strategies to achieve these goals becomes a valuable skill.

◊   Reflecting on the type of dance artist you aspire to be is a crucial decision; listen to your heart in this process.

◊   Learning various skills is not only enjoyable but also stimulates the growth of brain cells, making one smarter.

For example, if you want to learn choreography, it will be a great idea to establish and start your routine choreographic practice right away. Do not wait for someone else to ask you to choreograph a piece before you can start learning choreography. Your time is extremely valuable and limited, and **waiting could cost you precious time**. With or without a public performance scheduled in the near future, you can start to brainstorm the types of pieces you want to make. To take concrete actions, develop a short phrase or a piece for yourself or your dancer friends to practice and dance. You can encourage each of your friends to create a piece for others to dance as well. In this way, everyone gets the opportunity to learn choreography. It will be an exciting experience if you all can witness each other dancing the movements full-out! Remember to encourage and support each other's creative endeavors during this process. To make sure you practice regularly, consider setting a designated time to create a different phrase every (other) week. Keeping a journal to document your progress will help you stay on track with your practice.

If you are interested in making dance videos, videography will be a great skill to pick up. You can try to understand basic videography by watching online tutorials or checking out books from various libraries. If there is an in-person or online workshop that will teach you how to create videos or short films, don't hesitate to sign up. When you first start, it will be so much easier to create videos with a group of fellow artists. If you already feel comfortable recording your dance movements on a camera or smartphone, do it – so you can see them on a full screen instead of just peeping yourself in a mirror. Find ways to make this learning a fun and pleasant experience.

When establishing your learning schedule, the key is to take the initiative. If learning a new skill interests you, don't wait. Do your research and identify a list of steps you believe will help you learn. However, keep in mind that the goal here is not for you to become perfect in everything you do; perfectionism can sometimes do more harm than good. Rather than pursuing perfection, make this learning routine something you enjoy and look forward to. Integrate it into your long-term lifestyle and stay engaged and inspired. If you understand the purpose behind your learning and the "why" aligns with your interests and passions, it will undoubtedly help maintain your motivation throughout the learning process. Take action. Start your own learning today!

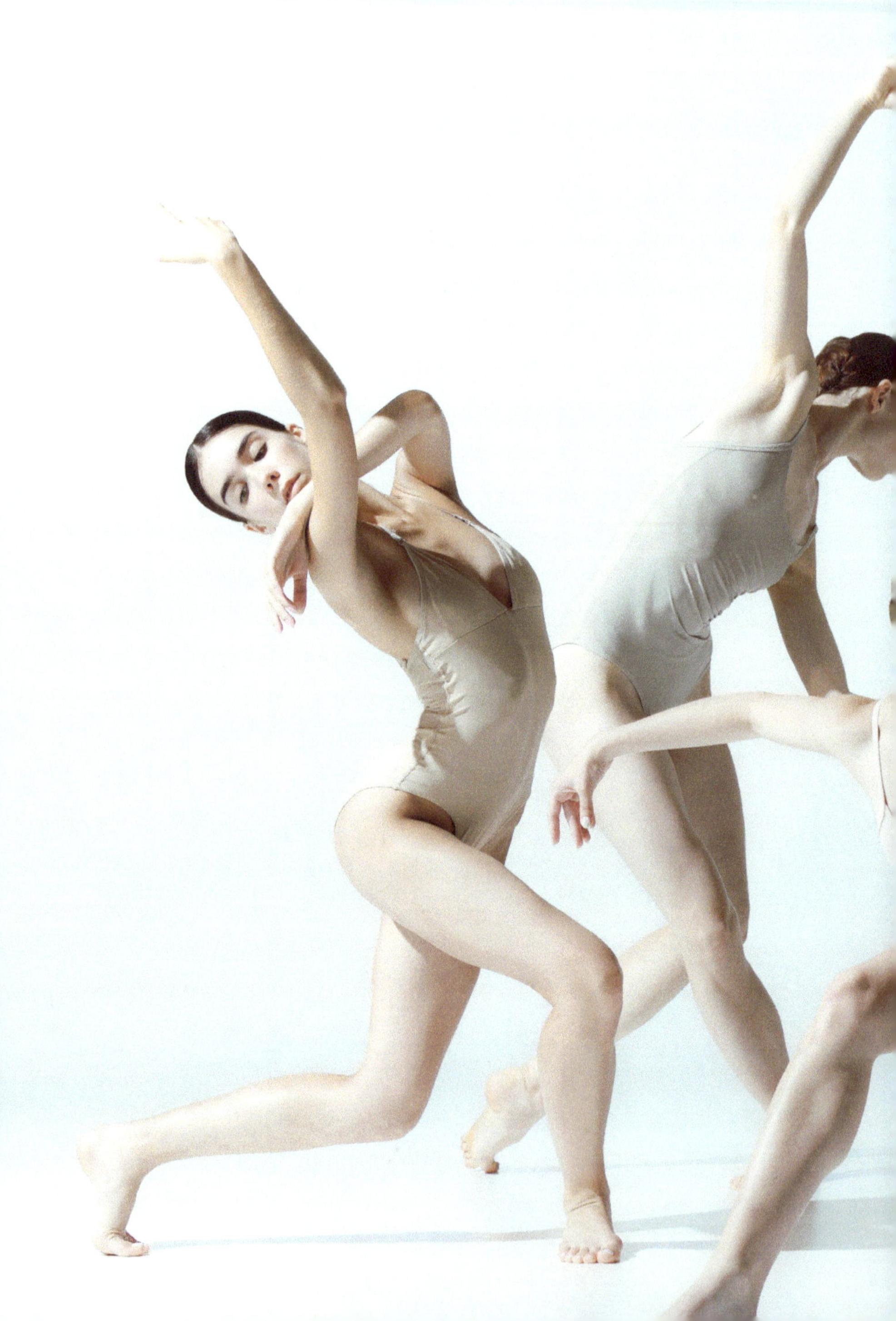

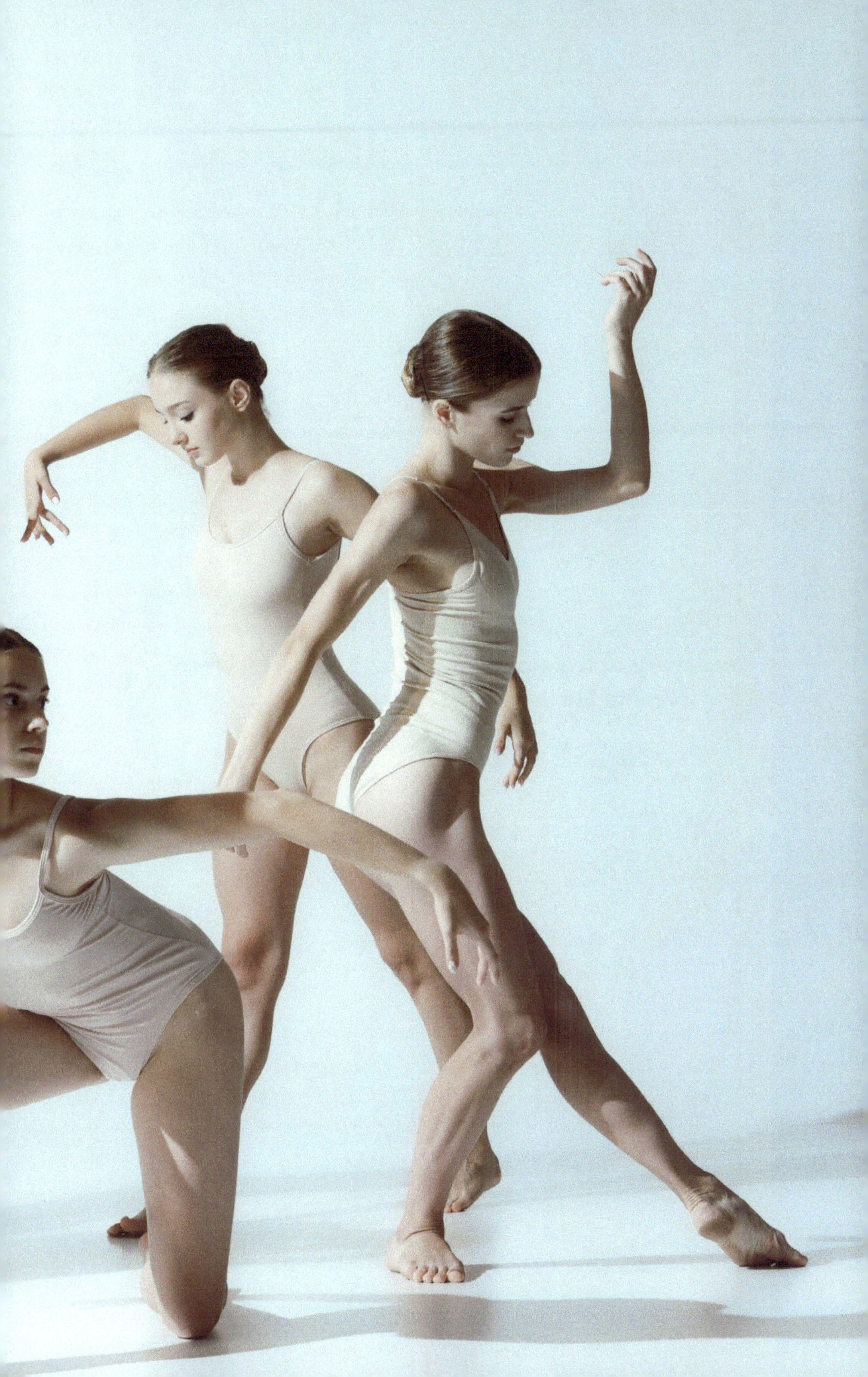

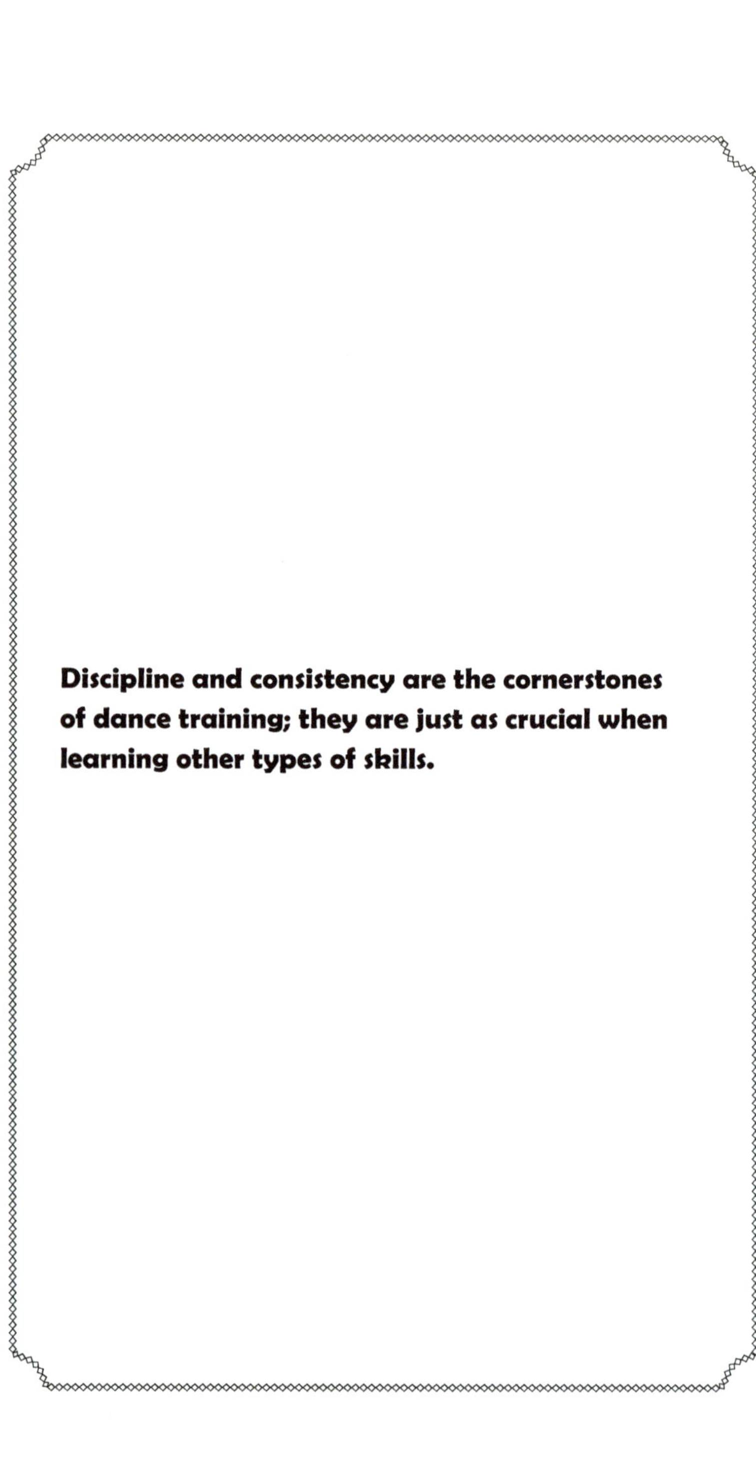

Discipline and consistency are the cornerstones of dance training; they are just as crucial when learning other types of skills.

9 Find Your Artistic Voice

One of the most amazing things about dance and art is that they allow us to express our feelings and tell our stories. Artworks are gateways for our artistic expressions and voices. Every dancer should find their unique artistic style. A deeply personal style is exceptionally precious because it encapsulates the essence of an artist's being. No matter how unconventional or quirky a dancer's style may be, it deserves to be seen and appreciated. Finding your voice in dance can be one of the most challenging yet exhilarating experiences in the journey to becoming a full-fledged dance artist.

American modern dancer and choreographer Martha Graham (1952) said, "There is a vitality, a life force, an energy, a quickening that is translated through you into action, and because there is only one of you in all of the time, this expression is unique. And if you block it, it will never exist through any other medium and it will be lost.

The world will not have it." Graham's quote captures the essence of why each of us should commit to uncovering and developing our artistic voices.

At the beginning of our dance journeys, many of us have role models. Perhaps you want to dance like Misty Copeland, or maybe you aspire to learn the iconic moves of Michael Jackson. Consciously or unconsciously, we may have tried to imitate our role models' artistic styles. By modeling ourselves after someone we admire, we get a taste of our early-stage artistic expression. This type of imagination gives us a glimpse of how it may feel once we fully develop our art. It is an amazing and beautiful feeling. However, as we mature as artists, the most important thing is not to become someone else but to **discover our own meaning and expression in art**.

Was there a particular piece of dance or artist that initially inspired you to become a dancer? How have they influenced your dance?

Your artistic voice should be something that you feel **deeply connected to**. It can be a style that empowers you, one that allows you to express your true self, or an expression that makes you feel connected with the universe, giving you a deep sense of purpose. The style that you choose can be refined and elegant, or it can be wild, edgy, and unorthodox. You can choose to develop multiple styles simultaneously, or you can choose to stick with your all-time favorite. There is no right or wrong; the only rule is that it is your style, and it should make you feel great about being an artist.

Ginger Davis Allman, a polymer clay artist and writer, has

advised on how to find one's artistic voice [15]. Allman's father, who became a sculptor at age sixty-eight, said that, at some point, you just have to "lean into it" and begin to make the art ***what you want, in the way you want it***. It will be the moment you stop imitating someone else and start to have your own style. By making your own choices, you may feel vulnerable or worry that you will fail to fit in with the people around you, but ultimately, you will see a style that is true, real, and authentic.

No matter your age or level of experience, there should be nothing that stops you from exploring your artistic expression. You will not need anyone's permission or approval before you can start developing your voice. Nobody is ever too young, too old, too stupid, or too smart to discover what types of artistic expression would resonate with their heart. You will never need someone else's approval to pick your favorite colors or choose your favorite songs. The same concept applies when searching for your artistic expression.

Our artistic voices will evolve over time. What empowered or represented us when we were young will certainly change when we grow into more mature artists. As we go through many phases of our lives, we will learn new skills, gain new wisdom, meet new people, and develop a new understanding of this world. Sometimes we will get the taste of sweet little victories, and sometimes we will inevitably experience the bitterness of failures. All these unique and valuable experiences will become part of our lives, influence our personalities, and ultimately be reflected in our art. So, even though you may already have your chosen style or expression, stay open-minded and flexible about it. Know that it will be completely healthy and normal if your artistic style evolves from its current state.

When it comes to finding our artistic voices, there is no single
correct answer. What's important is that we stay open-minded and
continue to make honest artistic choices that genuinely align with
our inner artistic aspirations. Whenever possible, we should strive
to remain brave and hungry for diverse life experiences; all these
encounters will one day serve as the nutrients for our artistic growth.
We should also try to look inside ourselves to reconcile our minds
with deep feelings and emotions. If we stay connected with ourselves
and with the world around us, our artistic voices will grow and flourish
naturally as we continue down our artistic journey.

15 Allman, G.D. (2022)

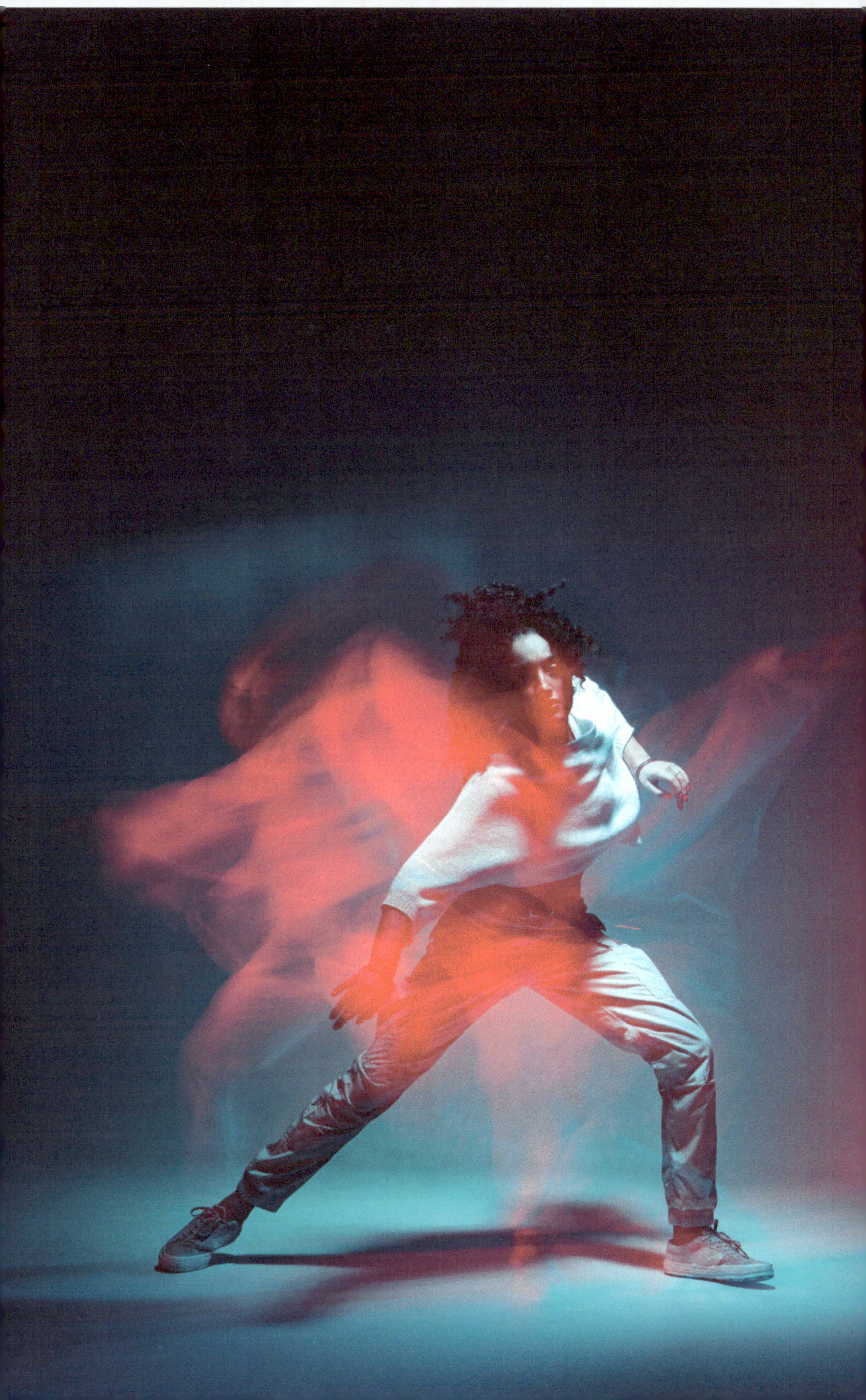

Has a real-life event, not directly related to dance, ever influenced or altered the way you moved or expressed yourself in art? Do you believe that profound life experiences will make an artist's work deeper and more powerful?

Dance Notes ~ write down your thoughts!

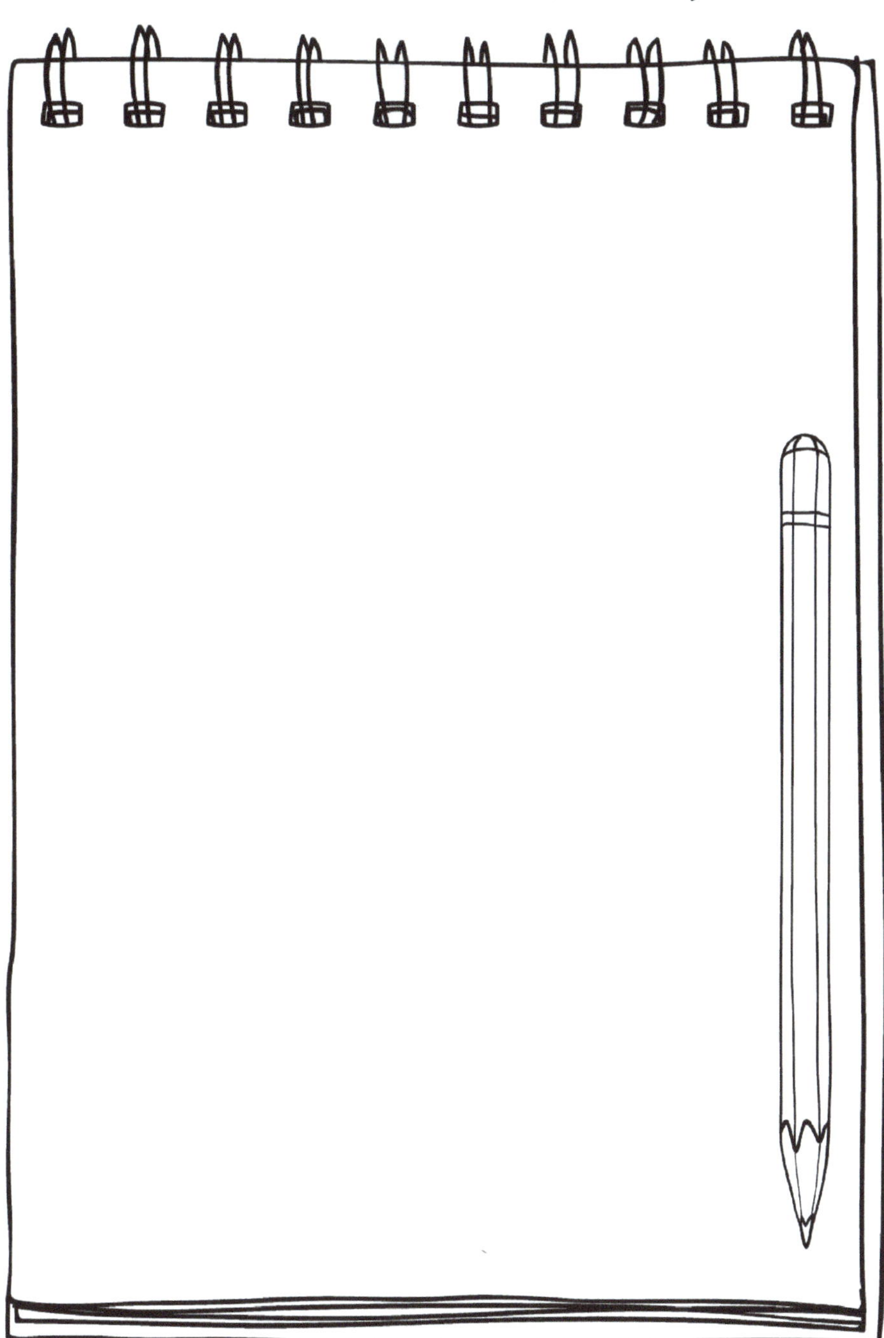

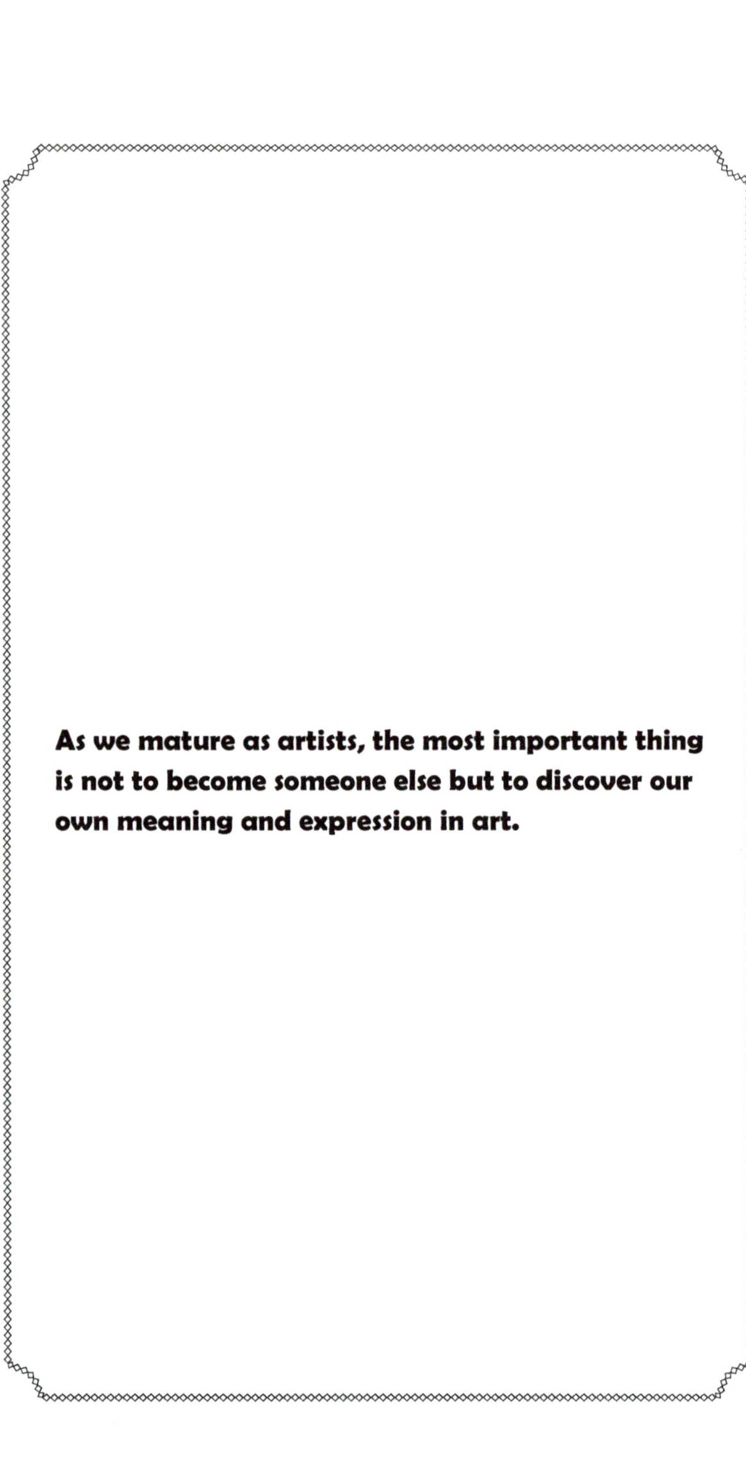
As we mature as artists, the most important thing is not to become someone else but to discover our own meaning and expression in art.

10 Body Inclusivity: Embrace & Love Your Body

As dancers, our bodies are instruments for art. We were born with different bodies. No two individuals in this world are ever entirely the same – even identical twins are rarely completely identical in their physical bodies and personalities. Because we all have distinct DNA and diverse upbringings, our bodies have different heights, sizes, shapes, skin colors, and features. Aside from our appearances, we also possess diverse personalities and gender identities, and our bodies have varying capabilities and limitations. All these differences are beautiful because they make each of us unique and irreplaceable.

Musicians can choose and switch between different musical instruments, and visual artists can choose their tools from a wide range of visual art mediums. Unlike musicians or visual artists, we dancers are born with the bodies we have from day one. As dancers, we can never exchange our bodies, whether we perceive them as ideal or not, irrespective of our health conditions. If we injure ourselves during a rehearsal or performance and persist in pushing through the pain, we risk jeopardizing our dance careers and, at times, our long-term health. As dancers, the last thing we want to do is put our bodies in harm's way. Our bodies have their natural ways of doing things, and going against these natural tendencies will not bring us any good results.

Are you satisfied with the look of your body and what it can do in dance? What are the reasons for your satisfaction or dissatisfaction?

Since each of us has only one body, which we are bound to have throughout our entire lives, there is one smart thing we can do: we should learn to **embrace and love our bodies!** A dancer's body is a one-and-only, powerful, irreplaceable, yet delicate, instrument for art. Before we try to train and challenge our bodies to the next level, it is crucial to first treat our bodies properly with acceptance, care, and love.

Accepting one's natural body type is not the same as passively giving up on rigorous dance training that always seeks to improve and achieve better results. This **acceptance of our bodies** is only the first step. It is the very foundation of our relationship with our bodies. Only when we take the first step correctly and have a true and harmonious relationship with our own bodies, will we be able to carry out ambitious plans in dance and continue to stay strong and healthy.

This is the only way we can make our dance learning and careers sustainable and continue to dance for many decades to come.

Art and creativity are fluid. A single story can often be conveyed in more than ten different ways through distinct sets of movements and styles. There is always more than one way to articulate a dance. That's where **creativity** comes in, and that's why art can never fail to surprise. As dance artists, we need to make wise choices about the types of movements we select and how we utilize our bodies. Only by doing so, will we discover the most effective ways to express ourselves in dance without causing unnecessary strains or injuries.

According to Valentini, an American journalist and writer, people in dance today are more aware of body inclusivity than ever before. Some dance professionals have been advocating for body inclusivity with their art and personal stories [16]. Erik Cavanaugh, a trained ballet, jazz, and contemporary dancer based in Nashville, was once told that he was "too big" to have a career in dance. Today, Cavanaugh's self-made dance videos have reached 570,000 followers on TikTok and Instagram. It is just one of the many success stories illustrating how a dancer can use their creative tools to combat body stereotypes and establish their unique brand in the competitive dance arena.

With creativity in dance, we can embrace body inclusivity while seeking our new definition of "beauty." What do you personally consider beautiful?

The idea of body inclusivity has grown prevalent in ballet as well. Gia Kourlas, the dance critic of The New York Times, once commented, "In ballet, line isn't just about the body's shape on a stage. It has to do with the body's overall harmonious outline: how, from head to toe, limbs and torso create the illusion of continuous reach and length [17]." We may not be able to alter the natural shapes of our bodies, and we shouldn't attempt to do so. However, with practice, individuals can learn to present their bodies in harmonious and continuous lines, achieving the elegant visual illusions sought after in ballet. What can help us as dancers is the thoughtful exercise of our bodies without forcing ourselves to do something that may cause discomfort or injury.

Art is rich and complex; there is so much more to it than a sheer number on a weight scale. When talking about **weight bias** in ballet, Benjamin Millepied, the former artistic director of the Paris Opera Ballet, said: "We've gone through a longtime trend of this idea of the skinny body, and I'm really against this. I want to see dancers who have their *individuality*." Audiences today are hungry to see dances that resonate deeply and meaningfully with their personal experiences. The art of ballet encompasses much more than the mere notion of skinny bodies moving within a stage frame.

Although we cannot forcefully make our legs grow a few inches longer or fundamentally change the shapes of our bodies, this does not mean that we should passively sit back. There are many good choices that we can make to better condition our bodies, so they can serve as articulative art instruments. When we properly protect our bodies and give them the right types of training and support, we can transform them into powerful artistic mediums that can express feelings and tell stories in dance.

Following are a few key points on how to make smart choices for our bodies and art:

Protect our bodies. One of the most important things we can do is to protect our bodies. Challenge the limits of our bodies *only when it is safe and healthy*. Know your physical limits. Recognize and assert your boundaries; don't hesitate to say "No" when someone asks you to do something that may hurt you. It is not always as easy as it sounds. Because of the intense competition in the field, dancers often strive to please the leadership of a dance organization or impress the audience – even if doing so may result in injuries. That's not worth it. Remember the saying, "It's better to be safe than sorry." A serious injury can easily take months, sometimes years, to heal, and it will most definitely jeopardize your long-term progress in dance. Speak up during rehearsals if certain movements bother you and communicate openly with your teachers or choreographers. Well-trained dancers should have the ability to communicate the capabilities or limitations of their bodies effectively, so the information can be considered carefully throughout the choreographic process. Providing early information about your body's capabilities or limitations allows choreographers to consider this and helps avoid movements that might cause harm.

Train smart. There is no one-size-fits-all training package. We are born with unique bodies and unique personalities. Because our bodies and personalities are different, it makes sense that each of us will benefit from different types of training. Try a diverse range of dance classes from different studios and instructors before deciding what works best for you. Be resourceful about finding the optimal mix of training for yourself. Listen to your body and don't hesitate to try out alternative exercises like yoga, Pilates, Gyrokinesis, weight training, or even Qigong and Tai Chi. Practices such as the Feldenkrais Method, the Alexander Technique, and somatic movement can sharpen our awareness of our bodies' conditions and improve our physical intelligence, sometimes bringing life-changing results. All these different training methods will work wonders for our bodies and minds.

Be creative in how you dance/perform. Because art and creativity are fluid, you can choose how you want to move. If performing a full pointe in ballet causes discomfort in your feet, try replacing the full pointe with a demi-pointe. If doing that deep backbend gives you a hard time, try a different gentle body bend with some expressive arm movement. Don't force yourself to move in a way that doesn't suit your body. If you can't enjoy the movement, the audience will not enjoy watching you. In the performing business, we all agree that "The show must go on." However, with creativity and a willingness to renovate and improve, there is always *a better way to articulate a dance*. Not only will they make the show go on, but these efforts will also enhance the quality of the performance. The beauty and fascination of dance lie in its flexibility and diverse ways of conveying expression, allowing each artist to find a unique and authentic voice in their movement.

Watch out for eating disorders influenced by distorted body images. A study published in 2013 found that as many as 16.4% of ballet dancers had suffered from eating disorders [18]. Eating disorders often affect young ballet dancers and artistic gymnasts, many of whom just begin their careers. The illness is commonly linked to a strict and rigorous perception of one's self image, along with feelings of dissatisfaction with oneself [19]. Unhealthy eating behaviors influenced by distorted body images can lead to serious health problems, including low energy, menstrual dysfunction, and low bone mineral density. Not eating enough food can hurt a dancer's ability to train, build strong muscles, and recover from injuries. Low bone mineral density increases the risk of **stress fractures** and even **osteoporosis**. In addition to making a dancer more prone to weak muscles, brittle bones, and painful injuries, eating disorders can also negatively impact a student's school performance. Research has found that eating disorders may cause difficulty with concentration, memory, mood control, and impulse control. In some cases, they can lead to anxiety and depression [20]. Eating disorders appear in various forms; some common ones are:

> » Anorexia Nervosa: A person has an intense fear of food and the possibility of gaining weight. They may go to extreme lengths to restrict or avoid food.

> » Binge Eating Disorder: A person eats an excessive amount of food in a short time and feels unable to stop.

> » Bulimia Nervosa: A person eats an excessive amount of food in a short time and then tries to rid the body of that food by self-induced vomiting, fasting, or exercising too much.

If you or someone you know is suffering from an eating disorder, having a conversation can be a good first step. Seeking professional help early is important, as it can shorten the duration of an eating disorder and reduce the damage it causes to the body and the mind.

Have a healthy lifestyle. It is no news that a healthy lifestyle is the key to sustainability in one's dance journey. Having sufficient sleep and a balanced diet will give your body the best chance to stay healthy. Now you know that a balanced and healthy diet is crucial for muscle building and can prevent injuries and osteoporosis - how about sleeping? Scientific evidence has shown that a lack of good-quality sleep will increase the risk of both **musculoskeletal pain** and **sports injury**. Researchers Huang and Ihm have discovered that when a lack of sleep lasts up to 14 days, the risk of musculoskeletal injury will increase by more than 1.7 times [21]! That's likely why dancers are particularly susceptible to injuries in the days leading up to an important premiere or performance event, when the chance of insomnia is high due to stress. Moreover, a study published in the Journal of Science and Medicine in Sport suggests that **sleep extension**, which is also known as "prolonged rest beyond the average sleep time", can help control inflammation and therefore accelerate recovery from muscle injuries [22]. When your body is healthy and strong, you have a much better chance of taking your dance performance to the next level.

Find a supportive community. Being surrounded by positive people helps us remain positive ourselves. Positive and creative friends will encourage body inclusivity and inspire us to **treat our bodies and art in the right way**. Sometimes we learn our best ideas from the people around us. Don't underestimate the influence that the environment can have on us. If the people around you aren't willing to support your dance style or judge you based on stereotypes, consider finding a different dance community that can serve as a more suitable home for yourself and your art. When caring for a delicate indoor plant, it's essential to place it in the most optimal spot within the house, where there is adequate fresh air and sunlight. As dance artists, we should take care of ourselves like how we tend to that delicate plant, fostering an environment where we can learn and cultivate our art to the fullest. We need to surround ourselves with kindness, support, and positivity, always.

16 Valentini, V. (2021, February 17)

17 Kourlas, G. (2021, March 3)

18 Arcelus, J., Witcomb, G.L., Mitchell, A. (2013, November 26)

19 Leonkiewicz, M. & Wawrzyniak, A. (2022, April 11)

20 Lampert, J. (2024, June 26)

21 Huang, K. & Ihm, J. (2021, June)

22 Chennaoui, M., Vanneau, T., Trignol, A., Arnal, P., Gomez-Merino, D., Baudot, C., Perez, J., Pochettino, S., Eirale, C., & Chalabi, H. (2021)

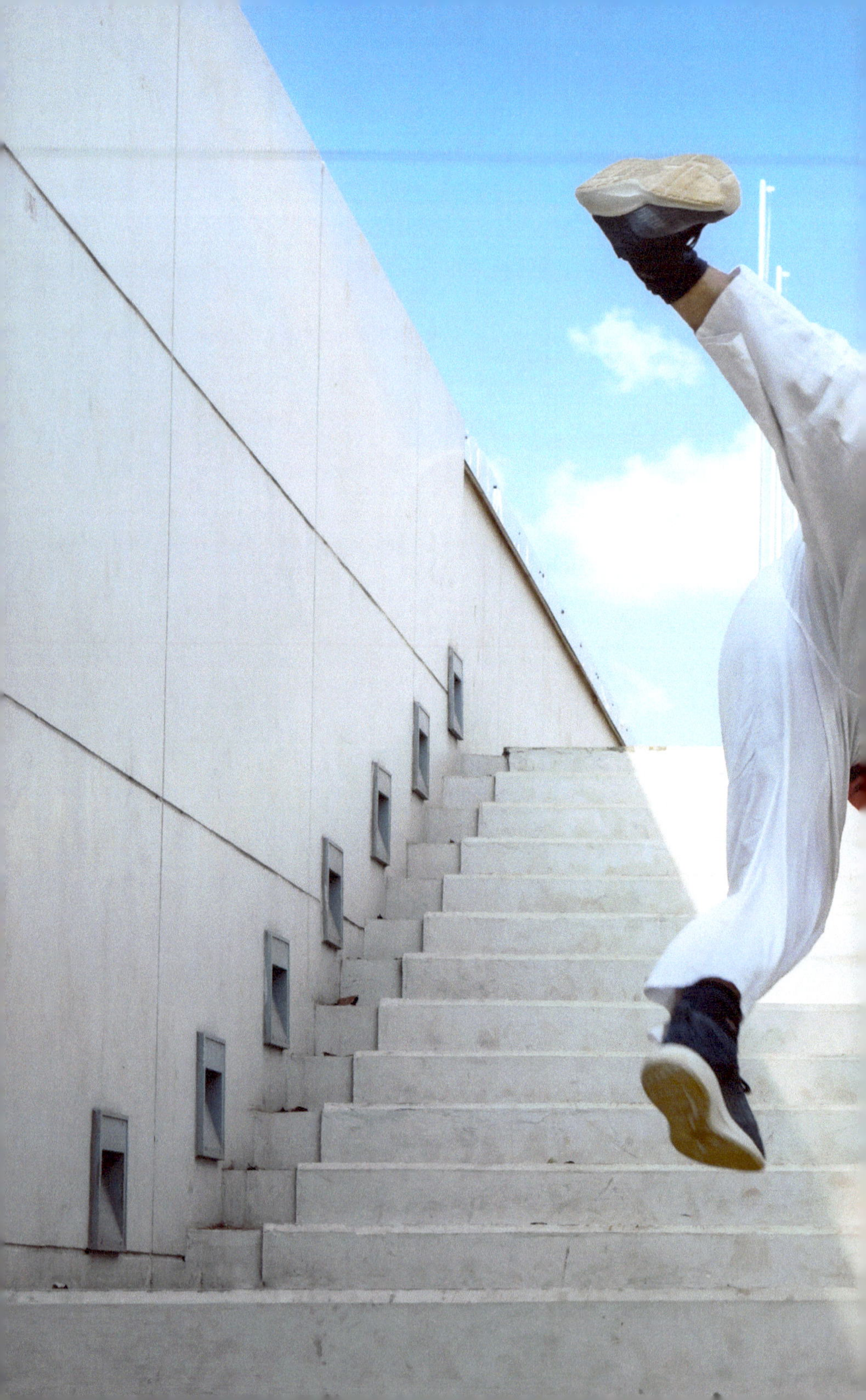

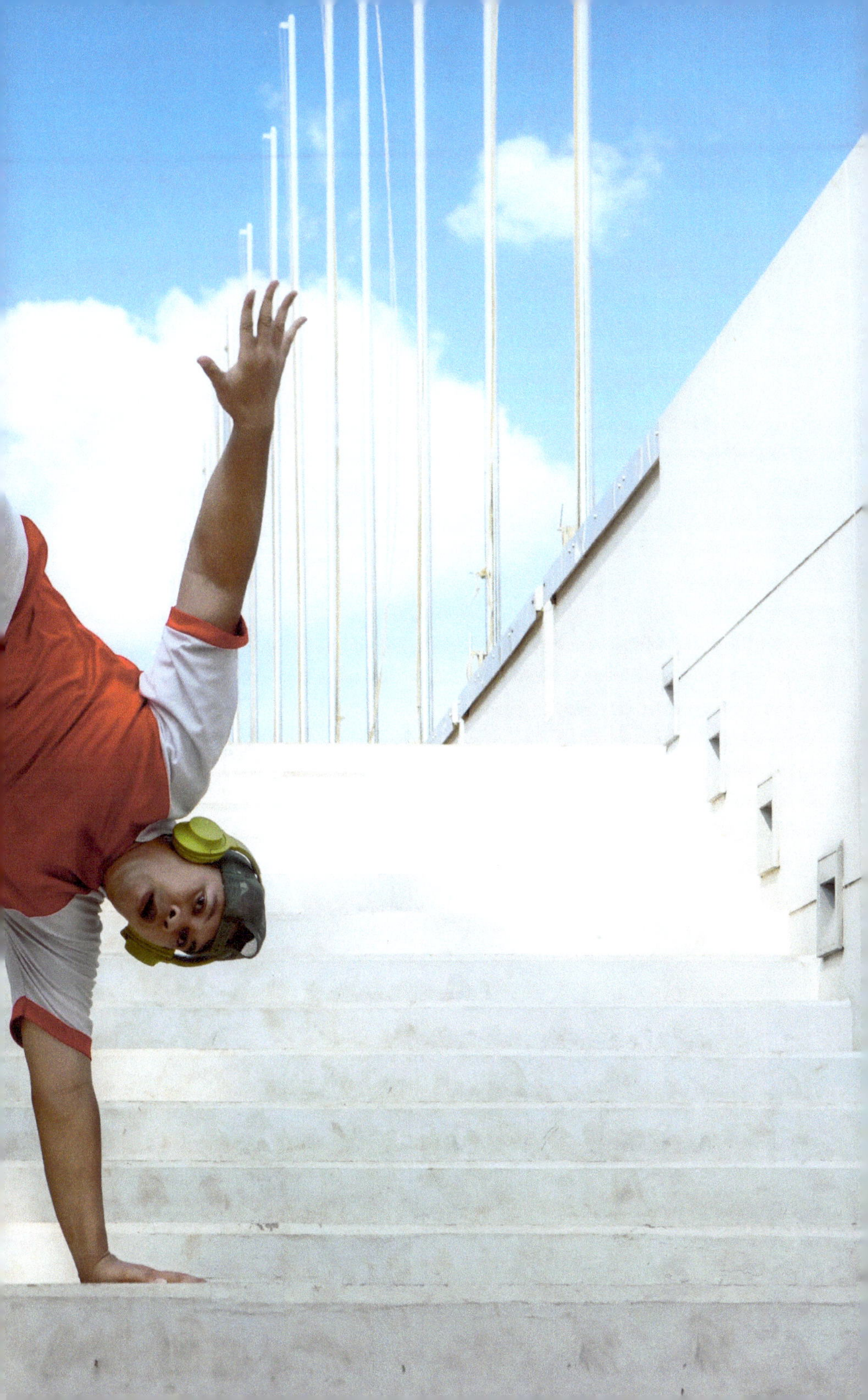

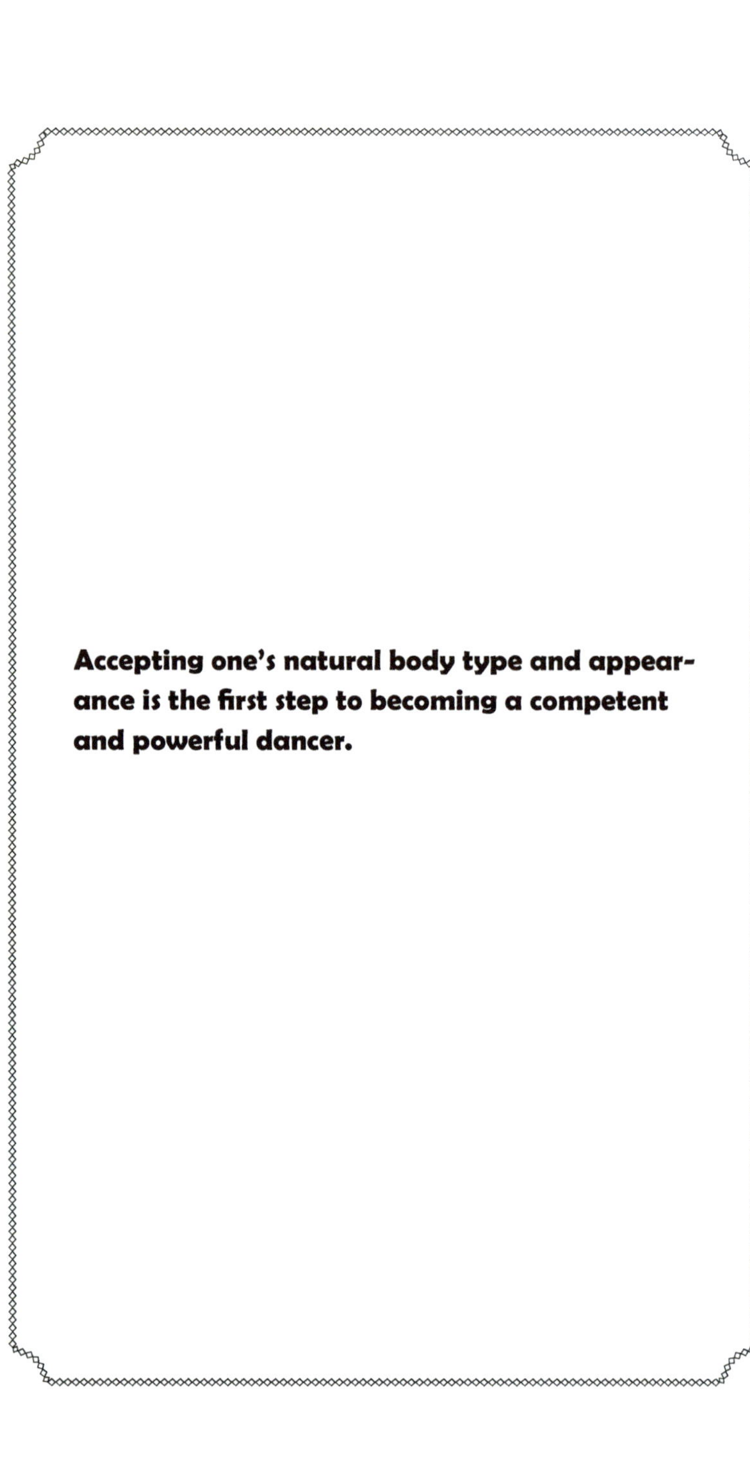

Accepting one's natural body type and appearance is the first step to becoming a competent and powerful dancer.

11 What Are Your Dance Goals

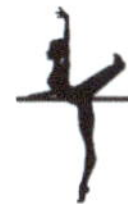

For those passionate about dance, there are hundreds of different ways to pursue a career in dance or to incorporate the art into our lives. If you haven't decided what you want to do with dance, it may be beneficial for you to ask yourself that question now. You can have one or multiple dance goals, and you are free to change or update your goals as you progress through your life. Your choices are personal. Like most things in art, there are no wrong ways to set your dance goals. You can listen to other people's advice, but the decision is ultimately yours to make. This is your life, and you deserve to do something that will **make you happy**. Like Ms. Garret, the accomplished ballerina and author, once wrote, "The matter won't be if you are an artist or not, but if you are the person you want to be, even when you are away from the spotlights [23]."

Once you have gone through the process of thinking and reflection to define your dance goals, you can make plans that will help you achieve those goals. You will have a better idea about which skills may be more important for you and which ones are less relevant in comparison. If you already have a busy training schedule, knowing what is important will help you sort out and prioritize your daily practices. The planning will help you streamline your practice and allow you to focus on what matters most. Altogether, it will make your dance goals much more attainable.

Talking to people in your dance community may also get you helpful tips or information to achieve your dance goals. Consider talking to your dance teachers, mentors, fellow artists, family, friends and anyone willing to support you in dance. For example, if you want to become a dance critic or journalist, someone in the community may be aware of an internship opportunity at the press, offering you the chance to practice writing dance articles. If your goal is to teach dance, it will be a great idea to apply for a teaching assistant position at a dance studio in your neighborhood.

Clearly defining your dance goals and actively working on them will bring you a more in-depth perspective on these subjects. You will learn the requirements and challenges firsthand. After a while, you will find out whether you want to continue with the same goals, or you want to switch up your priorities. The process will help you better understand what you genuinely want. If your goals change, don't panic. Just think them through carefully and then start with your new plans. Don't worry too much about wasting time if you have to switch plans. Whatever research or learning you have invested in the process will only make you a more **versatile and resourceful artist**.

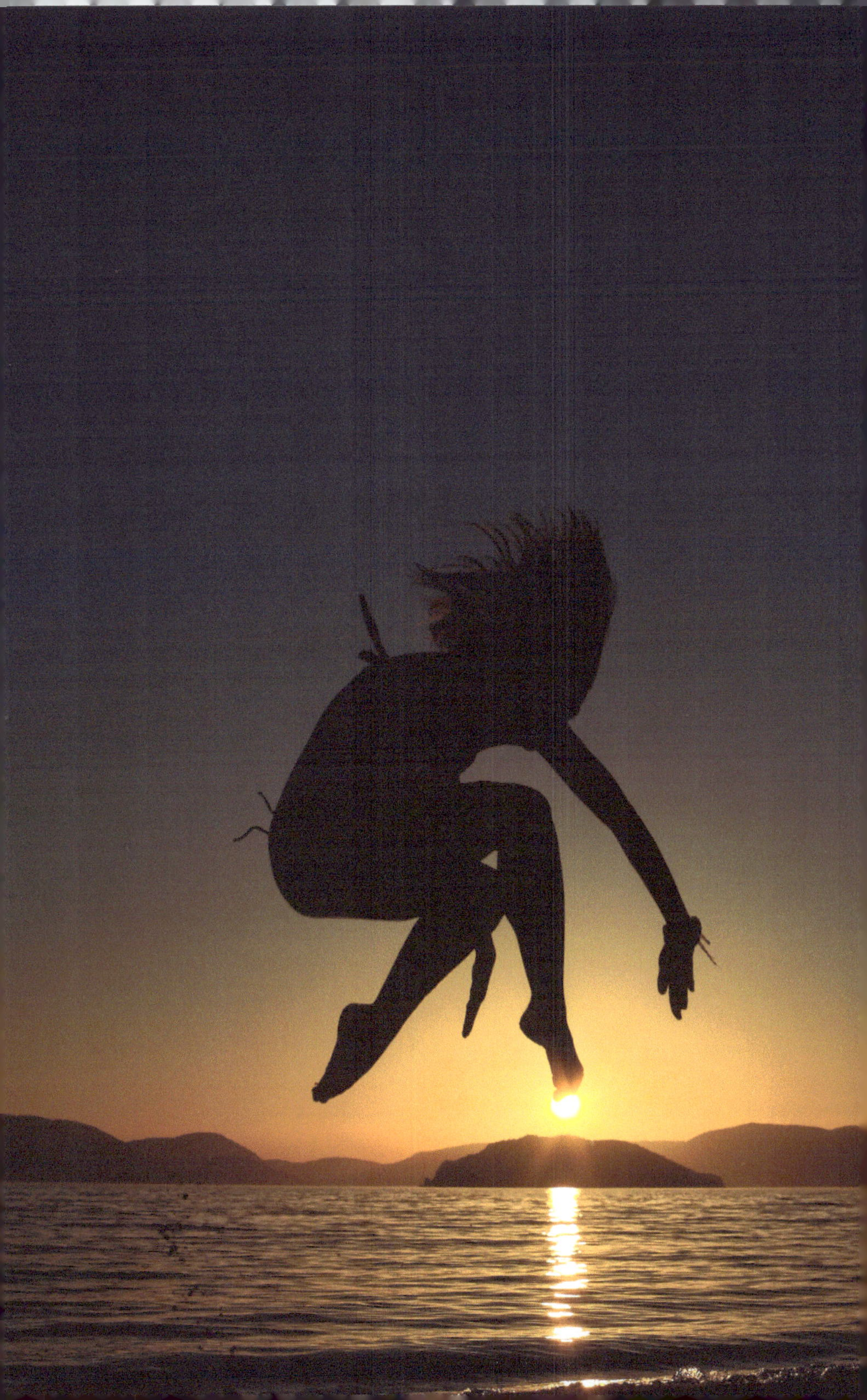

Write down three dance goals that genuinely excite you. (Yes, they have to be something that literally makes you smile from the heart!) Brainstorm some ways you could further yourself on these goals. Do you know anybody who could help you?

____

____

____

____

____

On the next page, you'll find a flowchart illustrating the cyclical nature of the goal-setting process in dance. Even after setting your goals, it's important to **_continuously re-evaluate your decisions_** through research and learning. "Reflection" is an important step as it's when you decide whether to stick with your current goals or make changes to them. Try to write down your thoughts and reasons for each decision in your dance journal.

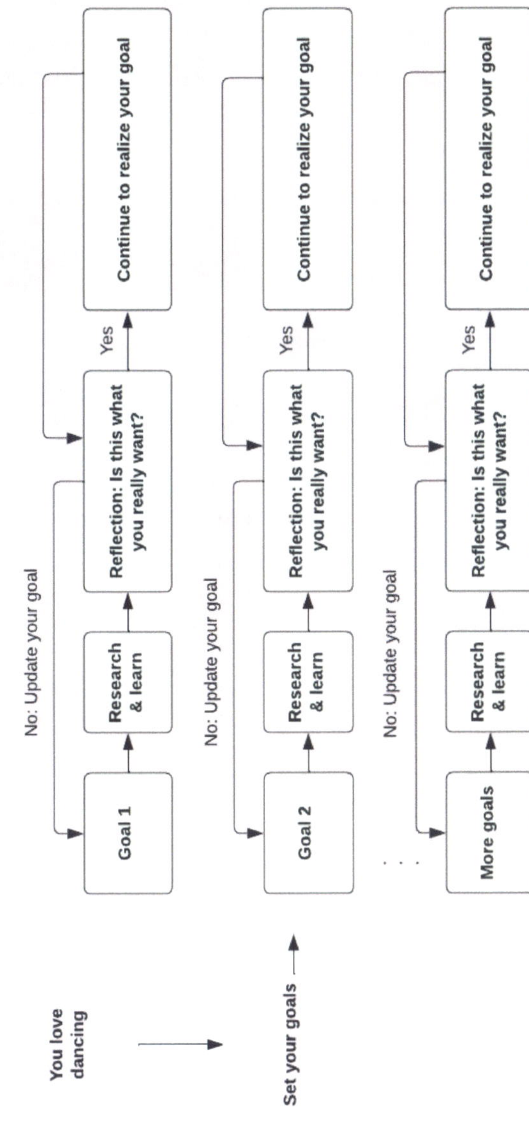

Figure 1 *The Cyclical Process of Goal Setting, Learning, and Goal Realization*

Below are some examples of goals related to dance. As you can see, you have many choices. Select your goals from the group and prioritize at least two of them. If you have additional ideas, feel free to add your own. Be as creative and imaginative as you can in envisioning and setting your dreams. As always, creative thinking is gold in art!

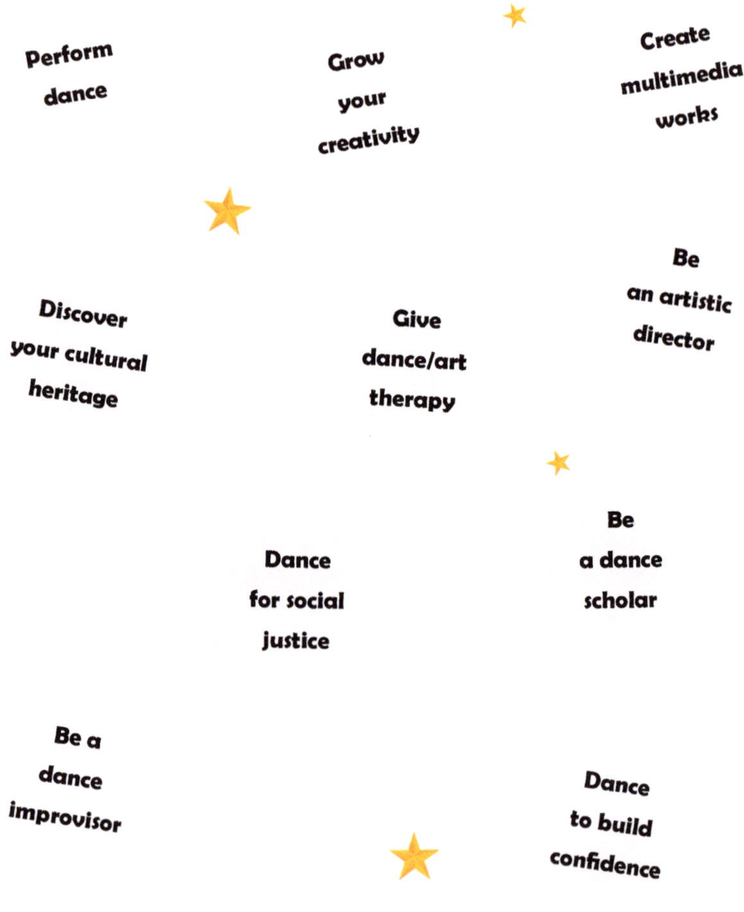

Back
up a dance
community

Make
experimental
dances

Be a
freelance
dancer

Teach
dance

Dance
to
enjoy life

Choreograph
new
works

Write
dance
blogs

Dance
to express
yourself

Dance
to
heal

Be a
dance
journalist

More idea:
____

More idea:
____

More
ideas ...
____

If you haven't started yet, it's time to create your plans and make your dance dreams come true. Don't hesitate to seek advice and support from your dance teachers and communities; they can be real treasures to guide and sustain you on your journey. Happy dancing!

---

23 Garret, M. (2021)

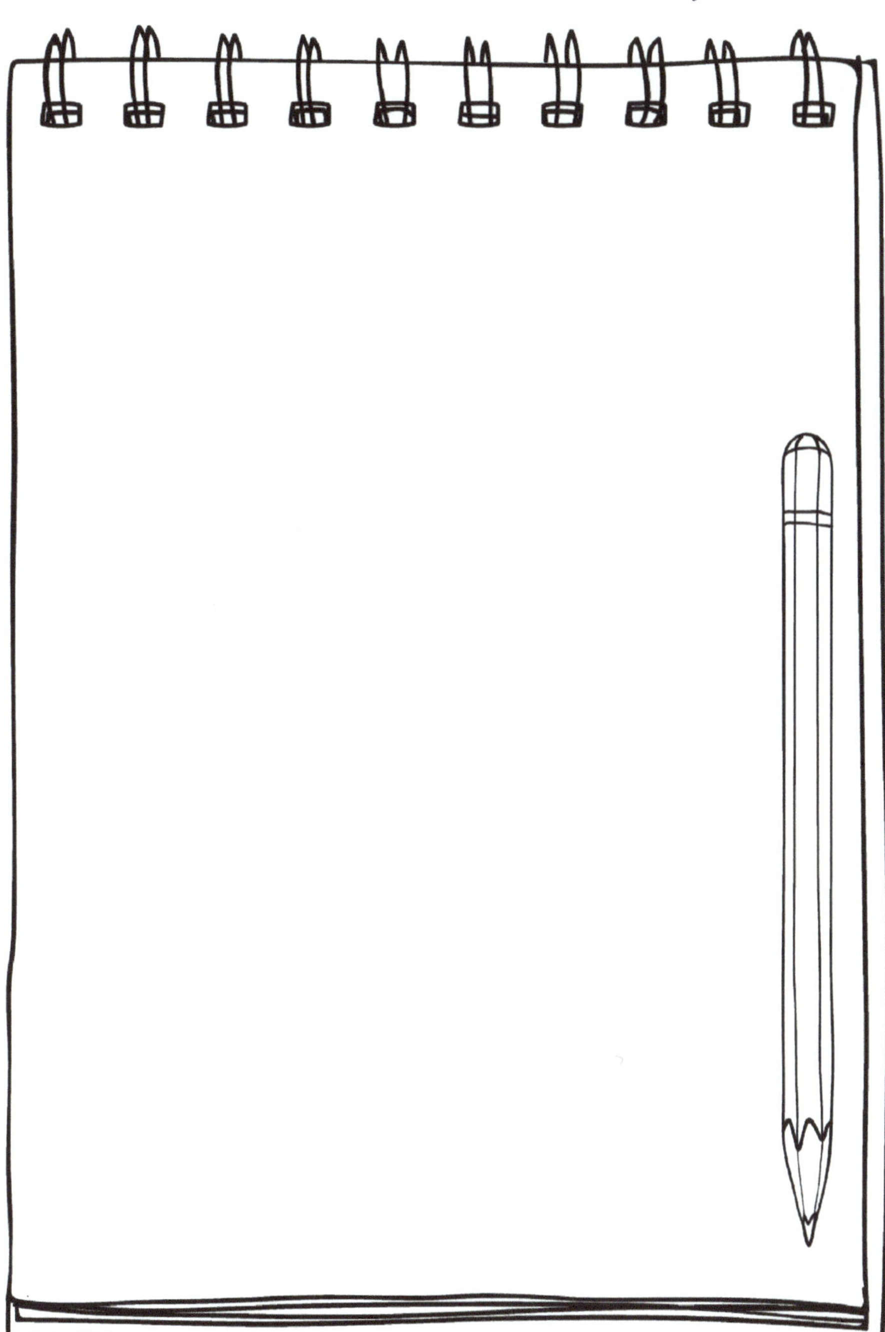

Dance Notes ~ write down your thoughts!

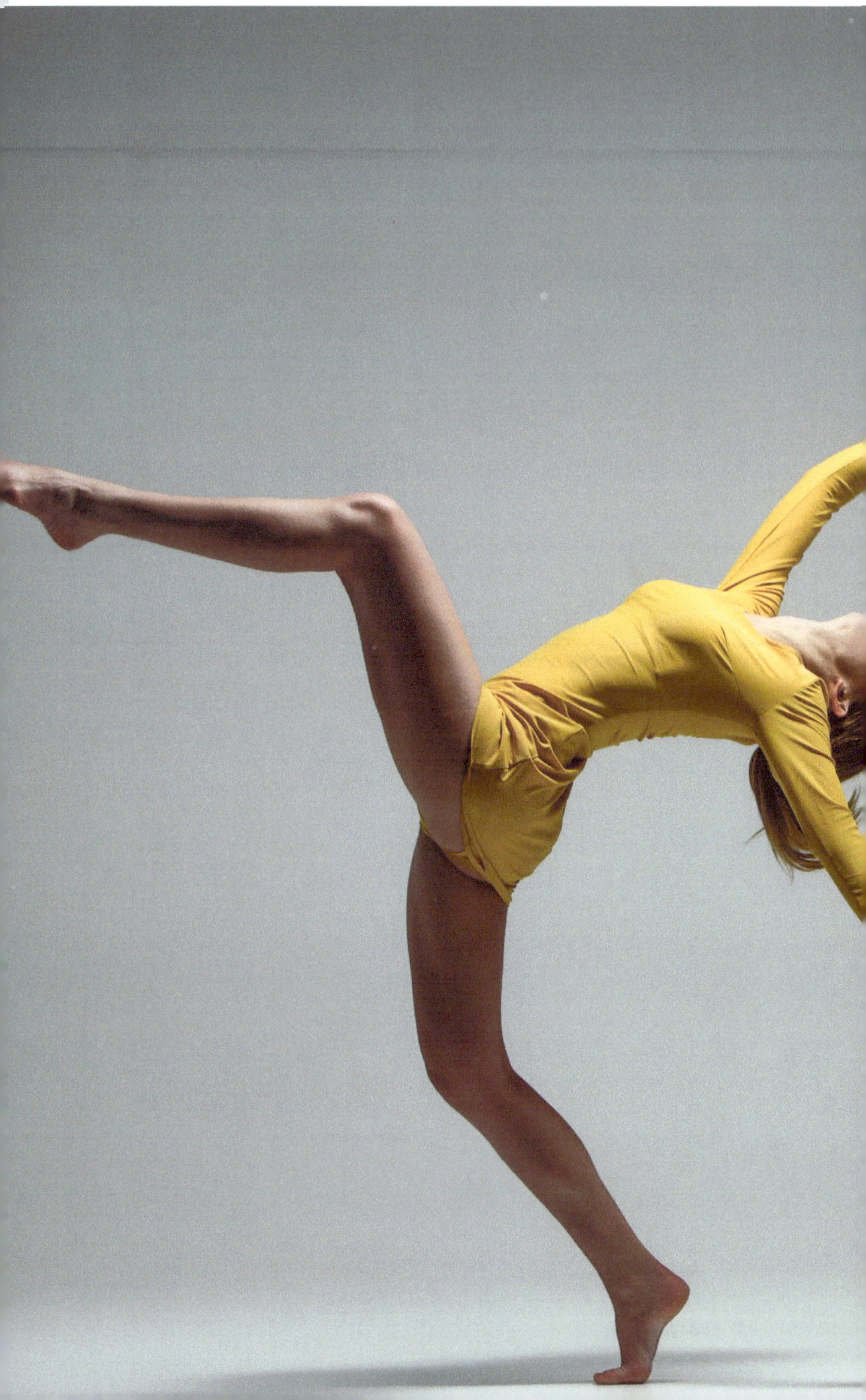

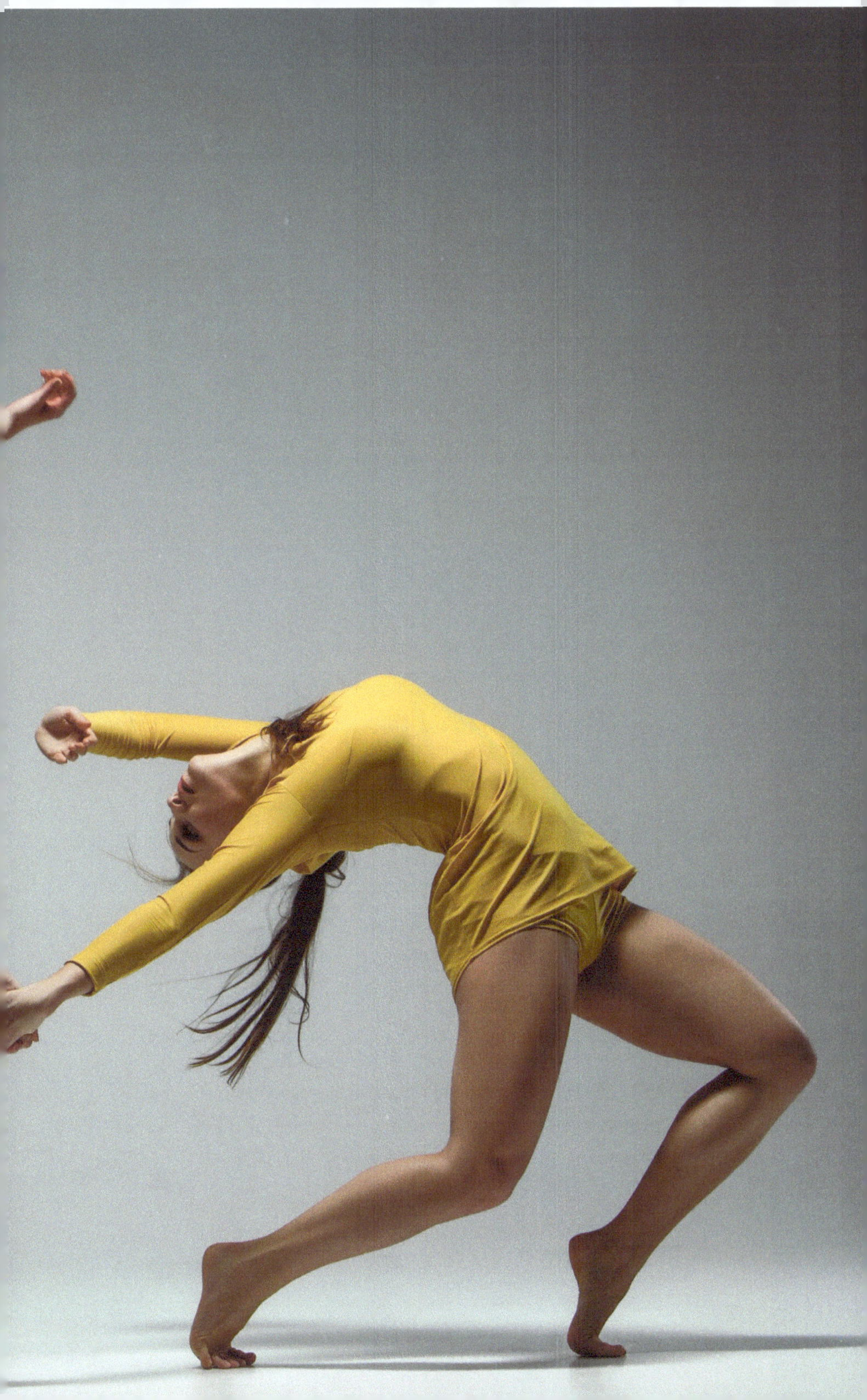

References

Allman, G.D. (2022). How Do You Find Your Artistic Voice? *The Blue Bottle Tree.* https://thebluebottletree.com/find-your-artistic-voice/

Arcelus, J., Witcomb, G.L., Mitchell, A. (2013, November 26). Prevalence of Eating Disorders amongst Dancers: A Systemic Review and Meta-Analysis. *European Eating Disorders Review.* https://doi.org/10.1002/erv.2271

Batson, G. & the IADMS Dance Educators' Committee (2009). Somatics Studies and Dance. https://iadms.org/media/3599/iadms-resource-paper-somatic-studies-and-dance.pdf

Blom, L.A. & Chaplin, L.T. (1988, December 15). *The Moment Of Movement: Dance Improvisation.* University of Pittsburgh Press.

Carter, C. L. (2000). Improvisation in Dance. *The Journal of Aesthetics and Art Criticism*, 58(2), 181–190. https://doi.org/10.2307/432097

Chennaoui, M., Vanneau, T., Trignol, A., Arnal, P., Gomez-Merino, D., Baudot, C., Perez, J., Pochettino, S., Eirale, C., & Chalabi, H. (2021). How does sleep help recovery from exercise-induced muscle injuries? *Journal of Science and Medicine in Sport*, 24(10), 982–987. https://doi.org/10.1016/j.jsams.2021.05.007

Dou, X., Jia, L., and Ge, J. (2021). Improvisational Dance-Based Psychological Training of College Students' Dance Improvement. *Frontiers in Psychology*, 12, 663223. https://doi.org/10.3389/fpsyg.2021.663223

Editors of Encyclopaedia Britannica (2023, March 26). Vincent van Gogh.

Encyclopedia Britannica. https://www.britannica.com/biography/Vincent-van-Gogh

Fujita, K., Gollwitzer, P.M., and Oettingen, G. (2007, January). Mindsets and pre-conscious open-mindedness to incidental information. *Journal of Experimental Social Psychology,* 43(1), 48-61. https://doi.org/10.1016/j.jesp.2005.12.004

Garret, M. (2021). *The truth, please, about ballet!*

Huang, K. & Ihm, J. (2021, June). Sleep and Injury Risk. *Current Sports Medicine Reports,* 20(6), 286-290. https://journals.lww.com/acsm-csmr/Fulltext/2021/06000/Sleep_and_Injury_Risk.3.aspx

Kourlas, G. (2021, March 3). What Is a Ballet Body? With performances on pause, many dancers are rethinking their relationship to weight. *The New York Times.* https://www.nytimes.com/2021/03/03/arts/dance/what-is-a-ballet-body.html

Lampert, J. (2024, June 26). Understanding the Impact of Eating Disorders on the Brain. https://emilyprogram.com/blog/eating-disorders-and-the-brain

Leonkiewicz, M. & Wawrzyniak, A. (2022, April 11). The relationship between rigorous perception of one's own body and self, unhealthy eating behavior and a high risk of anorexic readiness: a predictor of eating disorders in the group of female ballet dancers and artistic gymnasts at the beginning of their career. *Journal of Eating Disorders.* 10, 48 (2022).

https://doi.org/10.1186/s40337-022-00574-1

Morejón, J.L. (2021). Dance improvisation research: embodied self-esteem and self-confidence through glass art. *Research in Dance Education*, 21(2), 174-189. https://www.tandfonline.com/doi/abs/10.1080/14647893.2020.1746258?journalCode=crid20

Peters, U. (2022). What Is the Function of Confirmation Bias? *Erkenntnis*, 87, 1351-1376. https://doi.org/10.1007/s10670-020-00252-1

Powers, A. (2018, December 7). *Connecting the Dots: The Link Between Innovation and Open-Mindedness, With Insights From Science.* https://www.forbes.com/sites/annapowers/2018/12/07/connecting-the-dots-the-link-between-innovation-and-open-mindedness-with-insights-from-science/?sh=5b8140e77295

Rambert, M. (1972). *Quicksilver: The autobiography of Marie Rambert.* Macmillan.

Ravn, S. & Høffding, S (2022). Improvisation and thinking in movement: an enactivist analysis of agency in artistic practices. *Phenomenology and the Cognitive Sciences*, 21, 515–537. https://doi.org/10.1007/s11097-021-09756-9

Sehgal, K. (2017, April 25). Why You Should Have (at Least) Two Careers. *Harvard Business Review.* https://hbr.org/2017/04/why-you-should-have-at-least-two-careers

Schwarm, B. (2023, April 16). The Rite of Spring. *Encyclopedia Britannica.*

https://www.britannica.com/topic/The-Rite-of-Spring

Valentini, V. (2021, February 17). *Professional Dancers Advocating for Body Inclusivity*. https://www.shondaland.com/inspire/a35523202/professional-dancers-advocating-for-body-inclusivity/

Weir, K. (2022, April). The science behind creativity. *Monitor on Psychology*, 53(3). https://www.apa.org/monitor/2022/04/cover-science-creativity

Image Credits

Arija. Ballet dancer, aerobics, gymnastics . Vector illustration. Page 5.

Chaossart. Young man break dancing. Photo. Page 25-26.

Creativa Images. Dancer wearing hat and headphone doing handstand. Photo. Page 91-92.

Georgii. Cool dancing modern girl moving in colorful neon studio light. Photo. Page 78.

Gmm2000. Hand drawn notebook and pencil cute line art. Vector illustration.

Jockermax3d. Woman in dance pose against a wall outdoors. Arched ancient structure with cracked gray plaster outdoors. Photo. Page 63.

Konradbak. Stylish dancers facing in a concrete area. Photo. Page 45-46.

Lustre. Ballet school, dance education. Photo. Page 71-72.

Lustre. Two ballet dancers in an art performance dance isolated over a dark background. Photo. Page 8.

Mariia. Children dancing street dance silhouettes. Vector illustration.

Master1305. The two modern ballet dancers. Photo. Page 103-104.

Oneinchpunch. Dab dance on colored backgrounds. Photo. Page 55-56.

Smoxx. Sunset and silhouette. Photo. Page 95.

Svet_nn. Slim sportive young woman doing fitness and yoga exercises. Vector illustration.

Viacheslav Yakobchuk. Flexible ballet dancer stretching in the dark lighted studio. Photo. Page 37-38.

Vitaliy Mytnik. The girl in flight, white silk in the air. Photo. Front cover and Page 19-20.

All images sourced from Adobe Stock.

About the Author

Joyce Liao is a dance artist, choreographer, improviser, and writer whose practice spans contemporary and traditional dance forms. Her works often explore the intersection of movement and language, shaped by a deep interest in creative inquiry. She holds a BA in Dance from the University of Washington and has contributed to the local dance community through original choreography, improvisation, site-responsive performances, and interdisciplinary collaborations. Her works have been presented at venues including On the Boards, Velocity Dance Center, Studio Current, UW Meany Hall, Seattle Art Museum, Good Shepherd Center, Washington Hall, the Burke Museum, Hedreen Gallery, and others.

In 2012, during her creative residency at Studio Current, Liao expanded her skills in dance analysis, reflective writing, and creative writing through her involvement in Plumage, Walleye, and other artist-led practices. These experiences laid the foundation for her approach to writing about dance—one rooted in observation, dialogue, and creative inquiry. She also contributed performance reviews and cultural commentary as a freelance journalist for *Asia Today*, an experience that further shaped her voice as a writer.

Liao's current work focuses on exploring the poetic and holistic relationship between movement and creative writing. Through her work—on stage, on the page, and in community—she invites others to imagine what dance can be in the world we live in today: a practice for artistic expression, personal growth, and lifelong learning.